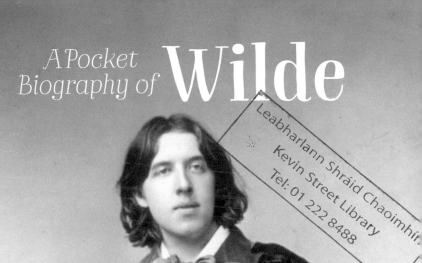

A Pocket Biography of Wilde

Gill Books
Hume Avenue, Park West, Dublin 12

www.gillbooks.ie

Gill Books is an imprint of M.H. Gill & Co.

Copyright © Teapot Press Ltd 2018

ISBN: 978-0-7171-7945-9

This book was created and produced by Teapot Press Ltd

Written by Fiona Biggs
Designed by Tony Potter

Printed in EU

This book is typeset in Garamond & Dax

A CIP catalogue record for this book is available
from the British Library.

5 4 3 2 1

A Pocket Biography of Wilde

Fiona Biggs

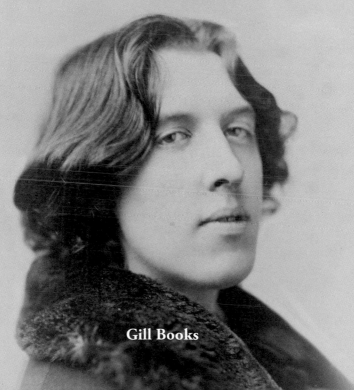

Gill Books

Contents

6   Chapter 1: The Wilde Family

22   Chapter 2: Oscar's Early Life

40   Chapter 3: An Oxford Man

56   Chapter 4: Making His Mark

74   Chapter 5: An American Lecture Tour

92   Chapter 6: Oscar in Paris

106   Chapter 7: Finding a Wife

124   Chapter 8: Marriage and Family

144   Chapter 9: The Picture of Dorian Gray

158   Chapter 10: The Playwright

176   Chapter 11: Lord Alfred Douglas

194   Chapter 12: Oscar's Trials

210   Chapter 13: Incarceration

228   Chapter 14: Exile and Death

246   Chapter 15: Oscar's Legacy

255   Select Bibliography

256   Picture Credits

Experience is the name everyone gives to their mistakes.

CHAPTER 1

The Wilde Family

After a good dinner one can forgive anybody, even one's own relations.

Oscar Wilde's childhood home in Merrion Square, Dublin.

Oscar Wilde was born in Dublin on 16 October 1854, the second child of William Robert Wills Wilde and Jane Francesca Agnes Wilde (née Elgee).

Oscar Wilde's father, the youngest child of Dr Thomas and Amelia Wilde, was born near Castlerea in County Roscommon in 1815. His paternal ancestors included a Colonel Wilde, a soldier in the army of William of Orange, who came to Ireland as part of the invasion force in 1689. William Wilde was educated locally in Roscommon, then he decided to follow in his father's professional footsteps. In 1832 he was apprenticed as a surgeon at Dr Steevens' Hospital in Dublin, and in 1837, after five years of study, he graduated from the Royal College of Surgeons in Ireland.

Instead of embarking on the European tour that was so popular with the young gentlemen of the day, the newly qualified Dr Wilde went on a cruise of the Mediterranean with a convalescent patient, exploring much of the coastal territories, including the Holy Land and Egypt. He was a polymath, interested not just in medicine, but in zoology, archaeology and folklore – in the course of his travels he dissected porpoises that landed on the deck of the ship and, after an examination of Egypt's ancient riches, he recommended that one of Egypt's archaeological treasures, Cleopatra's Needle, be brought to Britain.

On his return to Dublin Wilde set himself up in medical practice, rising to great eminence as an eye and ear surgeon. He was skilled, fashionable and in high demand as a society surgeon, but he was also a philanthropist, treating his poorer patients for nothing. These patients often shared with him traditional fables and stories, many of which he collected for later publication. In 1844 he founded his own specialist hospital in Dublin, St Mark's Ophthalmic Hospital for Diseases of the Eye and Ear, the first of its kind

The Book of Life begins with a man and woman in a garden. It ends with Revelations.

Oscar Wilde's father, Dr William Wilde.

> The longer I live the more keenly I feel that whatever was good enough for our fathers is not good enough for us.

in Ireland, and in 1863 he was appointed oculist to Queen Victoria in Ireland, a position that was created for him.

William Wilde had a reputation for enormous physical and intellectual energy. The remarkable collection of antiquities that is now housed by the National Museum of Ireland was catalogued by him during his spare time. In 1841 he was appointed medical commissioner to the Irish census. He wrote prodigiously, particularly in the field of medicine, and was a contributor to the *Dublin Journal of Medical Science* and, from 1845, its editor.

Sir William remained a bachelor until his mid-30s, but in 1838 he fathered a natural son, Henry Wilson, and in 1847 and 1849 a different mother gave birth to two daughters, Emily and Mary Wilde. Their father acknowledged all three children,

Sir William Robert Wills Wilde (1819–1876), Doctor, Antiquary and Father of Oscar Wilde, Erskine Nicol, 1825–1904.

provided for their support and had them raised by his relatives. The fact that his daughters were brought up by his older brother, Ralph, a minister of religion, gives an insight into the liberalism of the Wilde family. Sir William paid for Henry Wilson's training as a surgeon, not only in Dublin, but also in Paris, Vienna, Heidelberg and Berlin. Henry eventually returned to Dublin to join his father's thriving surgical practice.

Sir William's appearance was unremarkable, apart from an oily complexion that made him seem permanently grubby. Despite the success of his practice in higher echelons of society, his manners were generally regarded as somewhat unrefined. An anecdote doing the rounds in Dublin had the wife of the Lord Lieutenant refusing to eat her soup at a dinner hosted by Wilde, after the good doctor had tested the contents of the tureen with his finger.

However, the eminent surgeon was certainly a good enough match for Jane Frances Agnes Elgee, the youngest child of a lawyer and a member of the Anglo-Protestant ascendancy, with whom he fell in love and married in 1851. She was born in 1821 (she frequently lied about her age, knocking off as many as five years if the lighting conditions were sufficiently flattering, and generally letting it be known that the year of her birth was 1826), and at the age of 30 would already, by the standards of the times, have been gathering a heavy layer of dust on the shelf of spinsterhood.

Jane Elgee's background was populated with churchmen and physicians (and a bricklayer from as far back as the early 18th century) – her great-grandfather on her mother's side had been a physician and friend of Jonathan Swift. She was an unusually well-educated woman, an accomplished linguist (she spoke fluent French, German and Italian and translated numerous works of fiction, history and philosophy) and a committed suffragist and Irish nationalist. She collected and published ancient Irish 'charms and superstitions', and wrote stirring poetry supporting the nationalist cause under the pen name Speranza,

Jane Elgee

13

All women become like their mothers. That is their tragedy. No man does. That's his.

which means 'hope' in Italian (she made much of her Italian ancestry and provoked considerable mirth in the social circles of Dublin and London by claiming descent from Dante).

She contributed nationalist poetry to *The Nation* under the pseudonym John Fanshaw Ellis, and when the editor of that journal, Charles Gavan Duffy, was accused of authorship of some of her pieces that were troubling to the authorities, she announced from the public gallery at his trial that 'I, and I alone, am the culprit, if culprit there be!' Gavan Duffy was acquitted and Speranza dined out for some time on this tale of her heroism. She took over the editorship of *The Nation* in 1848 and was vociferous in her criticism of the potato famine that was then devastating the population of the country.

Jane Wilde has been described as a handsome and stately woman with flashing brown eyes, and she was certainly statuesque, at just under six feet in height. She was taller than her average-sized husband, and Victorian cartoonists made much of the disparity. While she was statuesque in her youth, as she gained weight in her later years she became enormous. Her appearance was decidedly eccentric – she wore dresses, headgear and jewellery that were generally considered to be excessive. As she got older she became reluctant to be seen in daylight, rising after midday and keeping the curtains in her house drawn at all times. She loved to be noticed and her mode of dress was also a manifestation of her rejection of bourgeois respectability. She deplored respectability: 'You must never employ that description in this house,' she once remarked. 'It is only tradespeople who are respectable. We are above respectability.' She was given to flamboyance, in her person as well as in her writing, and replaced her middle name, Frances, with the more exotic Italian version, Francesca.

Like his wife, William Wilde also espoused nationalism, expressed in his love of the Irish countryside and his fascination with the legends and fables of ancient heroes. In 1864 he built a house, Moytura, in Cong, County Mayo, on the site of a legendary battle between the Formorians and the Tuatha De Danann. His knowledge of folklore so impressed a visiting Swedish dignitary that he invited Wilde to Sweden in 1862, where he was conferred with the Order of Chevalier of the North Star.

After their marriage the Wildes moved into 21 Westland Row in Dublin city. Their first child, called William after his father, but always known as Willie, was born in September 1852. His mother had great ambitions for him, as a parliamentarian, perhaps, or even as the first president of her hoped-for independent Ireland. Just over two years later, Willie's younger brother Oscar was born, in October 1854. Jane Wilde described him to a friend as 'a babe of one month old … and as large and fine and handsome and healthy as if he were three months. He is to be called Oscar Fingal Wilde. Is that not grand, misty, and Ossianic?' The additional names O'Flahertie and Wills were added later. Jane always pronounced her second son's given name as if the second syllable were accented – 'Oscawr'.

Oscar was baptised the following April by his father's brother Ralph, the same Reverend Wilde to whom the care of all three of William's natural children had been entrusted. Two months later, Oscar's mother was describing the baby as 'a great stout creature who minds nothing but growing fat', in stark contrast to his tall and slim older brother. Jane is said to have hoped for a daughter rather than a second son. She is reported to have told a friend that she dressed and treated him as a daughter for the first 10 years of his life. However, Jane was given to hyperbole and outrageous statements, and this one is as likely to be true as her claim to descent from Dante. Oscar was sent to boarding school at the age of nine, dressed as a boy, and, in any event, the Victorian and Edwardian middle and upper classes dressed their sons as girls during the first years of their lives. The photograph of Oscar at the age of four, ringleted and wearing a sashed dress, is evidence of nothing except conformity to societal norms.

The longed-for daughter, Isola Jane Wilde, was born in 1857, some months before Oscar's third birthday, and she is said to have delighted the whole family. According to her mother, she had 'fine eyes and promises to have the most acute intellect.

To lose one parent may be regarded as a misfortune; to lose both looks like carelessness.

These two gifts are enough for any woman'.

William and Jane Wilde were loving and engaged parents – William enjoyed the daily company of his three legitimate children, and Jane revelled in her role as 'La Madre', convinced that at least one of her offspring would be a genius.

In 1855 the Wildes moved to the much more fashionable address of 1 Merrion Square, not far from the house at Westland Row. It was a house large enough to require at least six servants, and it was so much more desirable an address that Jane often urged the adult Oscar to say that he had been born there, which would have necessitated knocking two years off his age.

The new house was the perfect hub for entertaining the family's wide circle of friends, which included the fashionable

Oscar Wilde, aged four.

intellectuals and artists of the day, at lavish dinner parties. William Wilde was a generous host and a witty raconteur and his wife had a fine intellect and an exuberant and engaging personality. The house became one of the most fashionable gathering places in Dublin. When the dinner parties were largely replaced by Saturday afternoon 'at homes', they usually attracted upwards of a hundred people. Number 1 Merrion Square was *the* place to be and to be seen.

The Wildes's lifestyle was expensive, but William's busy practice was doing very well, so money came easily. However, he was a spendthrift, with no bent for economy. He became involved in several building projects – as well as Moytura House in County Mayo, he decided to build four small houses in Bray, County Wicklow, a popular 19th-century tourist resort near Dublin. He also bought a hunting lodge, Ilaunroe, on an island in Lough Fee, County Galway.

In 1864 William Wilde was knighted, not for services to medicine, but for his work as medical commissioner to the Irish census. The new Lady Wilde revelled in the family's social elevation (as did the nine-year-old Oscar), and it must have seemed as if the family's position and standing was at its zenith. However, shortly after he was knighted, Sir William found himself at the centre of a scandal. A patient of his, Mary Travers, claimed that he had raped her while she was under sedation for a surgical procedure. As the alleged crime had been committed two years previously and Travers had not left Wilde's practice, her chances of a successful criminal prosecution were slim. However, she wrote letters to the press impugning the surgeon, and even published a scurrilous pamphlet about Wilde and his wife. Jane Wilde was incensed, and, in an eerie harbinger of the events that would unfold in Oscar's life, she sued Travers for libel. Lady Wilde lost the case, although only a farthing was awarded in damages, and she was left with a legal bill for the enormous amount of £2,000. Although Sir William's friends and colleagues took his part in the affair, his reputation was damaged and it was the beginning of the end of the happy and prosperous life enjoyed by the Wildes.

George Morosini, 1840–1882.
Jane Francesca Elgee, Lady Wilde (1821–1896), writer, (Pen-Name *Speranza*) and mother of Oscar Wilde.

CHAPTER 2

Oscar's Early Life

Children begin by loving their parents. After a time they judge them. Rarely, if ever, do they forgive them.

Oscar had a happy, carefree childhood. The Wilde boys did not attend a preparatory school, but were educated at home by their parents and a procession of German, English and French governesses. They had access to their father's vast, eclectic and well-organised library and to their mother's enormous collection of works of literature. Holidays were spent at Moytura House or at Ilaunroe, swimming and fishing in Lake Fee. It was on these holidays that Oscar first heard and became enthralled by the old Irish legends and fairy tales that so fascinated his father. Although he was a keen reader and loved beautiful books, Oscar enjoyed the Irish oral tradition of storytelling and throughout his life regarded narration as the superior vehicle.

The children even participated to a degree in their parents' social life – during dinner parties they were allowed to sit at the end of the table, although in keeping with the Victorian motto

Scene at Moytura House. Oscar Wilde on far right.

that 'children should be seen and not heard', they were not allowed to speak on these occasions. However, even at a young age, the precocious Wilde boys must have absorbed some of the content of the witty intellectual and political conversation that flew back and forth across the dinner table.

Jane Wilde remained convinced that she had mothered a genius – Willie was the focus of her attentions in this regard, although his general disobedience and lack of application to his lessons at home caused him to be sent away to boarding school in May 1863. The school, St Columba's College in Rathfarnham, in the South County Dublin countryside, was

Youth is the one thing worth having. To get back one's youth, one has merely to repeat one's follies.

not so very far away from home, but it didn't suit Willie's temperament, and in February of the following year he was sent to the newly opened Portora Royal School in Enniskillen. Nine-year-old Oscar was sent with him – by then, his mother was beginning to realise that it was her younger son who might live up to her high expectations. He spent seven years at Portora, although he once stated in an interview that he had been tutored at home.

Shortly after the boys began their school career at Portora, William Wilde received his knighthood. Oscar thereafter referred to his father as 'Sir William' in his correspondence with his mother. Although news of his father's involvement in the subsequent Travers scandal must have made its way to the school, Oscar never mentioned it in his letters home.

Portora Royal School in Enniskillen.

At Portora the masters, like Jane Wilde, thought that Willie was the clever brother – he had the quick family wit, was very good at drawing and was also a tolerable pianist. The headmaster told Oscar that, with some effort, he might emulate his older brother. Oscar soon began to confound expectations – he was a natural and highly talented speed-reader, absorbing the detail of entire novels in just a few minutes. He was also beginning to demonstrate the wit that would later make him famous. However, he studied only those subjects that interested

him, Greek and Latin most particularly, ignored anything to do with science and loathed mathematics. His astounding ability in the subjects that engaged his interest led to his being exempted from the annual examinations in 1866.

By now, Oscar was tall for his age, with a large build and a dislike of all sporting activities. His classmates and masters remembered him as slovenly and dirty, and perhaps he was, in the manner of many young boys, but he was already demonstrating the dandyism that would become his trademark; he wore his hair long and his favourite shirts were unusually brightly coloured at a time when the convention was for white shirts worn with dark suits. He wrote to his mother that she had sent him the wrong shirts:

> The flannel shirts you sent in the hamper are both Willie's, mine are one quite scarlet and the other lilac ...

Both brothers were well regarded for their ability as raconteurs – at this point, Willie was better than it than Oscar, who could also amuse his classmates with his extraordinary double-jointed contortions.

The Portora pupils kept up with the news stories of the day, and an account of the trial of a vicar for heresy at the Court of Arches fascinated Oscar. He declared that he would like to 'go down in posterity as the defendant in such a case as "Regina versus Wilde".'

In 1867 tragedy hit the Wilde family when Isola died of a fever at the age of nine. William Wilde was devastated and Lady Wilde wrote to a friend that 'My heart seems broken. Still I feel I have to live for my sons and thank God they are as fine a pair of boys as one could desire.' Oscar was deeply affected by his sister's death. He is said to have carried a lock of her hair ever afterwards and he wrote a poem for her, 'Requiescat', the first verse of which was later inscribed on her headstone.

At Portora, Oscar shone ever more brightly with the passing years. In 1871 he was awarded a Royal School scholarship to Trinity College Dublin, and his name was added to the gilt-on-black school roll of honour – it was scraped off the board in 1895 when he was disgraced, although it was later reinstated.

Oscar's Trinity scholarship at the age of 16 should have been a cause for family celebration, but 1871 was yet another tragic year for Sir William. His two natural daughters, Mary and Emily, were both burnt to death when their dresses were set alight as they twirled in front of an open fire before leaving the house to attend a party. Their father, now bereaved of all three daughters, was heartbroken and went into a decline from which he never recovered. He neglected his medical practice and the family's financial fortunes, unbolstered by any wise investments, went into a downward spiral. The affluence the family had enjoyed during Oscar's childhood would gradually disappear.

Willie was already making his mark at Trinity when Oscar embarked on his undergraduate degree there a few days before his 17th birthday. Since so many of Dublin's intelligentsia had frequented their mother's salon, the Wilde brothers were already well acquainted with a number of the faculty members. The Professor of Ancient History, the reverend John Mahaffy, was one such, and he would have an enormous influence on Oscar. He was Oscar's tutor and mentor and the author of *Social Life in Greece* (published in 1874), which includes an apologia for 'Greek' love. He encouraged Oscar's interest in all things Greek, including the idea that relationships between older men and

Requiescat

Tread lightly, she is near
Under the snow,
Speak gently, she can hear
The lilies grow.
All her bright golden hair
Tarnished with rust,
She that was young and fair
Fallen to dust.
Lily-like, white as snow,
She hardly knew
She was a woman, so
Sweetly she grew.
Coffin-board, heavy stone,
Lie on her breast,
I vex my heart alone,
She is at rest.
Peace, Peace, she cannot hear
Lyre or sonnet,
All my life's buried here,
Heap earth upon it.

Musical people are so absurdly unreasonable. They always want one to be perfectly dumb at the very moment when one is longing to be perfectly deaf.

> Youth smiles without any reason. It is one of its chiefest charms.

youths were even more important than those between men and women. In later life Oscar would write that he was 'the scholar who showed me how to love Greek things'. Mahaffy was witty and erudite and he was also a lover of beautiful things, fine wines, travel and stimulating conversation, all of which would have appealed to the young undergraduate.

Trinity College is a five-minute walk from Merrion Square – the Wilde home was on the corner of the square nearest to the entrance gate – and Oscar lived at home for much of his time there. For a while he had rooms in the university accommodation block known as Botany Bay (it was located on the site of a vegetable garden that had been cultivated to supply the university). He loved to entertain guests in his sitting-room there, where he had set

The Long Room, Trinity College Library.

up an easel, complete with a half-finished painting (he later replicated this affectation in his rooms at Oxford). He had already developed an admiration for the Pre-Raphaelites and their sensual depictions of women, which had found favour with the public imagination in England. At Trinity Oscar could find few kindred spirits among his acquaintances and he began to feel that Dublin might be rather too provincial for his refined sensibilities. It was at Trinity that he first became acquainted with the concept of aestheticism, derived from poet and literary critic John Addington Symonds's interpretation of the Greek approach to morality. Trinity provided a course in aesthetics, and it was a subject frequently debated by the university Philosophical Society. Oscar later developed Aestheticism (with a capital A) into a philosophy that determined his entire approach to life.

It was at Trinity that the template for Wilde's life began to take shape. Jane Wilde, herself a prolific poet, had instilled in Oscar a love of poetry as the highest art form – his favourites were Spenser, Shakespeare and the Romantics, particularly Tennyson and Swinburne, and the American poets Longfellow

> To have been well brought up is such a great drawback nowadays. It shuts one out from so much.

and Walt Whitman. Encouraged by his mother he had penned many poems of his own, and while at Trinity he began to develop a serious interest in writing poetry. The nascent dandyism that had been exhibited in his dress at Portora became full blown and he began to strike the languid poses in which he was often photographed throughout his life. He also became interested in Roman Catholicism, probably attracted by its ritual and mystery rather than any of its theological differences with Protestantism. His mother had secretly had him baptised (for a second time) at St Andrew's Catholic Church in Westland Row when he was a small boy. Sir William Wilde was not enamoured of Catholicism, and although Oscar would flirt with the Roman religion throughout his life, he never converted. While his father was still alive he gave as the reason for his refusal a fear of being disinherited.

Although Oscar excelled academically at Trinity, winning the Berkeley Gold Medal for Greek and achieving outstanding results in his examinations, an academic career at Trinity was neither attractive to him nor a foregone conclusion. His tutor and mentor, Professor Mahaffy, thought that a spell at Oxford would be beneficial, and Sir William hoped that a move away from Ireland would cure his youngest son of his dalliance with Roman Catholicism, so it was decided that Oscar would go to

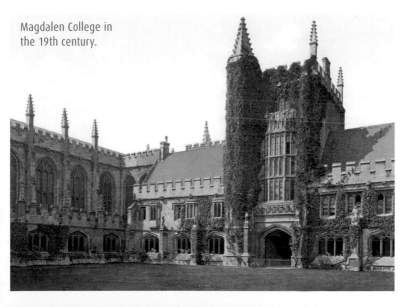

Magdalen College in the 19th century.

England. Willie was already there, training as a barrister in the Middle Temple in London.

In March 1874 Magdalen College at Oxford announced that it would award two scholarships (known as demyships) in classics (known at Oxford as Greats) that year. Candidates were required to prove that they were under 20 years of age and that they were of good conduct. Oscar was within the age limit by just a few months. In June Lady Wilde, increasingly convinced that Oscar, rather than Willie, might be the genius in the family, brought him to Oxford, where he presented his credentials and sat the examination. After being awarded one of the demyships – his marks were far higher than any of the other candidates – he celebrated with his mother and brother in London. They went on a holiday to Geneva and came back via Paris. It was Oscar's first visit to the City of Light. He said that it was while they were staying there that he began to write his dramatic poem 'The Sphinx' (first published in 1894), which was influenced by his reading of the dark writings of Edgar Allan Poe. It ends with the verses:

Get hence, you loathsome mystery!
Hideous animal, get hence!
You wake in me each bestial sense, you make me
  what I would not be.
You make my creed a barren sham, you wake
  foul dreams of sensual life,
And Atys with his blood-stained knife were
  better than the thing I am.
False Sphinx! False Sphinx! By reedy Styx
  old Charon, leaning on his oar,
Waits for my coin. Go thou before, and leave
  me to my crucifix,
Whose pallid burden, sick with pain, watches
  the world with wearied eyes,
And weeps for every soul that dies, and weeps
  for every soul in vain.

The old believe everything; the middle-aged suspect everything; the young know everything.

Oscar and Lady Wilde returned to Dublin to find that Sir William had gone into a decline. Supporting two sons in higher education was an expensive business, and in 1872 he had mortgaged their Merrion Square house. Some of Lady Wilde's jointure also had to be raided to cover the family's expenses.

Although Oscar was concerned for his father, he couldn't contain his delight at being awarded a scholarship to Oxford. He was congratulated and fêted by his friends and Professor Mahaffy joked, 'You're not quite clever enough for us here, Oscar. Better run up to Oxford.'

Caricature of Dr Sir WIlliam Wilde.

A
WILDE ESSAY
ON
PAT~OLOGY
—
BELFAST

CHAPTER 3

An Oxford Man

Education is an admirable thing, but it is well to remember from time to time that nothing that is worth knowing can be taught.

I n October 1874 Wilde booked his passage on the mail boat from Kingstown (now Dún Laoghaire) to travel to England to take up his Oxford scholarship. He was six foot three in height, with a large and somewhat ungainly build. He was also remarkable for his limpid blue eyes. His teeth protruded slightly and he had fallen into the habit of covering his mouth while speaking. While he was not handsome, he had presence, and his height, very unusual in the Victorian era, was guaranteed to draw attention wherever he went.

He began his studies at Magdalen College the day after his 20th birthday. Older than most of the other undergraduates, he had huge self-confidence. His Irish accent (a slight brogue, according to a contemporary account) marked him out, and he had soon disguised it: 'My Irish accent was one of the many things I forgot at Oxford.' He was soon declaring that Oxford was 'the most beautiful thing in England … the capital of Romance.' He dressed flamboyantly, developed a chain-smoking habit and kept company with the sons of the rich, up at Oxford more for the experience than for any learning that they might have absorbed. His interest in Roman Catholicism ebbed when, following a family tradition, he joined the Freemasons (William Wilde had been master of one of the Dublin lodges).

He was enrolled in the study of Greats, the very demanding honours course in Latin and Greek languages and literature. Oscar's knowledge of these subjects, achieved at Portora and Trinity, was such that he felt able to spend a good deal of his time on an extra-curricular study of modern philosophy and literature. He paid scant attention to his studies in his first term and failed his first examination, Responsions, in November of his first year. For someone who had shone

The only way to atone for being occasionally a little over-dressed is by being always absolutely over-educated.

academically up to now, this must have been a devastating humiliation. He applied himself to his studies in the privacy of his room, although outside them he pretended to an academic nonchalance that mirrored that of his friends. Throughout his life he railed against the concept of 'testable' knowledge as a stultifying approach to education, although he believed that during his time at Oxford Greats had not yet been subverted by the examination process.

Oscar's ability to speed-read meant that he could read and absorb a huge amount of information in a very short space of time. He had always amused people with his witty observations and now he began to collect material from which to craft them. He kept a commonplace book and several notebooks in which he jotted down quotations and ideas that particularly appealed to him. His apparently off-the-cuff remarks during conversation were refinements of ideas that he encountered in the course of his reading, fine-tuned and honed to perfection. These were the precursors of the epigrams that would give him enduring fame.

Thanks to his capacity for wit, Oscar was already becoming famous in the small and rarefied world of the university. His

Examinations are futile exercises in which the foolish ask questions that the wise cannot answer.

Wilde at Oxford, 1878

observation that he found it 'harder and harder to live up to my blue china', did the rounds of Oxford (several years later it even made an appearance in *Punch*). His love of beautiful things led to his magpie-like collecting of objects with which to furnish his rooms – his witty remark was a reference to two blue vases that he bought to hold the lilies that would become his floral emblem.

Oscar had been brought up in an affluent household where money was plentiful and ran easily through the fingers of his generous and hospitable parents. He carried on their tradition of hospitality at Oxford, entertaining lavishly in his rooms in Chaplain's Quad (he later carried on the practice in Cloisters and Kitchen Staircase). Following the tradition of his mother's Saturday 'at homes', he devoted Sunday evenings to an open house where large quantities of alcohol were consumed. The rules at Oxford at that time were strict, and frequently flouted by Oscar and his friends – students could not frequent places where alcohol or tobacco were sold, and they had to be in their rooms by 9.00 at night. Oscar's gatherings came within the letter of the law and must have been a welcome diversion. However, Sir William's decline had had a devastating effect on the family income – and with no experience of practising economy Oscar ran up huge bills with the local tradespeople, particularly the vintners and booksellers.

During the summer vacation after his first year at Oxford Oscar went to Italy with Professor Mahaffy, visiting Florence, Bologna, Venice, Verona and Padua. He wrote enthusiastic accounts to his father of everything he saw there and began to write poetry seriously (his writing from this period was published in his first volume of poetry). He had become interested in Renaissance art after attending a series of lectures given by John Ruskin, who later became his friend and mentor. By end of June the Italian adventure had depleted his cash reserves and he decided to spend the rest of the vacation in Ireland. He had not made it as far as the centre of Roman Catholicism and remarked on this in his poem 'Rome Unvisited':

> *And here I set my face towards home*
> *For all my pilgrimage is done*
> *Although, methinks, yon blood-red sun*
> *Marshals the way to holy Rome.*

That summer Oscar also spent some time at Moytura House and Ilaunroe, fishing and generally enjoying country life, and in August he returned to Dublin, where he became acquainted with Florence Balcombe, a 17-year-old from a military family. Their friendship was affectionate and that Christmas Oscar gave her a gold cross inscribed with both their names. However, the feelings they had for each other soon cooled and Florence later married the author of *Dracula*, Bram Stoker.

Oscar's wealthy friend Hunter Blair, a Scottish baronet, was his best friend at Oxford and an enthusiastic shopping companion. Like Oscar, Blair was interested in Roman Catholicism and he converted during a trip to Italy on that first long vacation in 1875. On his return to Oxford he tried to persuade Oscar to do the same, but although he was still attracted he was unwilling to make the commitment, despite ongoing pressure from Blair, who was exasperated when Oscar told him that he was as yet undecided as between Roman Catholicism and atheism. He was still concerned that he would be disinherited by his father's family if he converted: 'To go over to Rome would be to … give up my two great gods "Money and Ambition".'

While at Oxford, Oscar's interest in all things Greek was deepening. John Addington Symonds's commentary on the Greek classics, *Studies of the Greek Poets*, became his bible, and he was convinced, like Mahaffy and Symonds, that Greek philosophy had a direct connection to modern life. Oscar regarded one of the most important questions in life as 'What is good for man?' and found the answers in his study of the Greek writers, Plato particularly.

The mind of a thoroughly well-informed man is a dreadful thing. It is like a bric-à-brac shop, all monsters and dust, with everything priced above its proper value.

To know
everything
about oneself
one must
know all
about others.

Plato emphasises the spiritual nature of homosexual love, celebrating the love of an older man for a younger, a union that is referred to as 'paederastic'. Perhaps it was Plato who unearthed a latent tendency in Oscar, at a time when to act on that tendency was punishable by imprisonment. So-called 'boy worship' was in vogue in Oxford during Oscar's time there, and may have appealed to him. He certainly wrote poetry that was focused on beautiful boys. However, an acquaintance of his, William Hardinge, was sent down in 1876 for writing some homosexual poetry, and this may have been an object lesson for Oscar, who never made the mistake of bringing his own predilections to the attention of the college authorities.

Hardinge attracted the notice of the authorities when it was discovered that he had received several letters from Walter Pater that were signed 'Yours lovingly'. Pater was an Oxford don who exercised an enormous influence over Oscar. For the Victorians, morality was the driving force behind everything, including art. Pater's philosophy denied the requirement that art be moral. He believed in 'art for art's sake', an idea that found immediate resonance with Oscar, who was still formulating his own philosophy of aestheticism.

In 1877 Oscar went on an archaeological trip to Greece with Mahaffy during the spring vacation. He was more than three weeks late for the beginning of the Trinity term and justified his tardiness with the statement that 'Seeing Greece is really a great education for anyone and will I think benefit me greatly, and Mr Mahaffy is such a clever man that it is quite as good as going to lectures to be in his society.' The Dean of Arts was unimpressed and Oscar was sent down (rusticated) for the remainder of the term. Years later he remarked archly that he was sent down 'for being the first undergraduate to visit Olympia'.

He decided to go to Dublin for the duration of his rustication. Sir William had died on 19 April 1876, a much

A really well-made buttonhole is the only link between Art and Nature.

poorer man than he had once been, and Oscar's inheritance (the Bray houses and a share of Illaunroe) was not what he might have hoped for. He began to realise that he would eventually have to earn his living. En route from Oxford to Dublin, he visited a Pre-Raphaelite exhibition and wrote a review for the *Dublin University Magazine*. He enjoyed this first experience of having a work of prose published, and decided that he would like to be an art critic.

Back in Oxford that autumn, Oscar embarked on his final year of study. He was determined to achieve a brilliant result, and he did, being awarded a rare double first in his degree (in the 19th century only a handful of Magdalen undergraduates achieved a similar result). He also entered the competition for the prestigious Newdigate Prize for Poetry, sponsored by

Jane Burdon: detail of a Pre-Raphaelite drawing by Dante Gabriel Rossetti.

Sir Roger Newdigate, for the best piece of verse written by an Oxford undergraduate. The subject set for the competition in 1878 was the ancient city of Ravenna, in Italy, and Oscar drew on his own experience of visiting it when writing his winning entry. In his long poem in praise of the city he establishes himself as a poet in the mind of the reader.

Art is our spirited protest, our gallant attempt to teach Nature her proper place.

Ravenna, Italy: The magnificent domed Baptistry of Neon. *Jesus Christ being baptised by John the Baptist and around him the 12 apostles.*

O much-loved city! I have wandered far
From the wave-circled islands of my home;
Have seen the gloomy mystery of the Dome
Rise slowly from the drear Campagna's way,
Clothed in the royal purple of the day:
I from the city of the violet crown
Have watched the sun by Corinth's hill go down,
And marked the 'myriad laughter' of the sea
From starlit hills of flower-starred Arcady;
Yet back to thee returns my perfect love,
As to its forest-nest the evening dove.
O poet's city! one who scarce has seen
Some twenty summers cast their doublets green
For Autumn's livery, would seek in vain
To wake his lyre to sing a louder strain,
Or tell thy days of glory; poor indeed
Is the low murmur of the shepherd's reed,
Where the loud clarion's blast should shake the sky,
And flame across the heavens! and to try

Such lofty themes were folly: yet I know
That never felt my heart a nobler glow
Than when I woke the silence of thy street
With clamorous trampling of my horse's feet,
And saw the city which now I try to sing,
After long days of weary travelling.

I don't at all like knowing what people say of me behind my back. It makes one far too conceited.

His triumph of a warm reception at the public reading of the poem was somewhat tarnished by the extent of his debt to the Oxford traders. His mother, who had moved to London soon after Sir William's death, advised both her sons to overcome their financial difficulties by marrying rich heiresses. Oscar had other ideas.

Cartoon of Wilde in *Punch*.

CHAPTER 4
Making His Mark

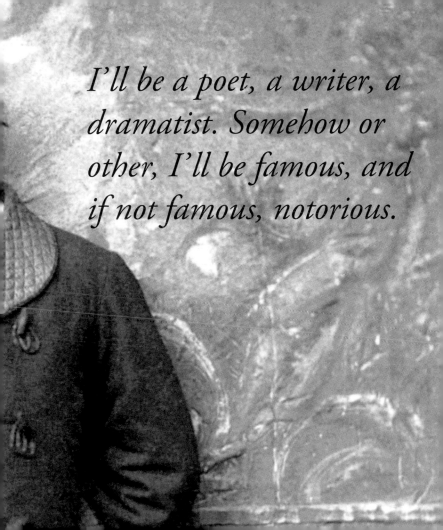

I'll be a poet, a writer, a dramatist. Somehow or other, I'll be famous, and if not famous, notorious.

The years Oscar had spent at Oxford must have made Dublin seem like a provincial backwater. Without the immediate prospect of a rich heiress to marry, as recommended by his mother, he knew that he would have to earn his living. Where better than the hub of artistic life, the capital of the British Empire? In the summer of 1876 Oscar moved to London, determined to make his name as a literary man. Willie was already living in London, and the recently widowed Lady Wilde was planning to make her home in the city she regarded as the 'capital of the world' (she moved there in 1879).

One of Oscar's friends, the artist Frank Miles, the son of a wealthy clergyman, had a house in Salisbury Street, off the Strand, a reasonably fashionable address that was conveniently close to London's theatres, art galleries and fine restaurants. Oscar moved in with Miles and proceeded to enjoy life to the full, dining out and attending the theatre and parties. He had studied hard at Oxford, but in the real world his parents' work ethic did not seem to have rubbed off on him. He lived as if he had a private income, but in reality he had very little money. He was witty, entertaining and stylish was therefore in great demand in fashionable drawing rooms. After his mother had moved to London the Wednesday and Saturday afternoon receptions at her salon in Mayfair were particularly good occasions for Oscar to be seen and practise his witty repartee. The Prince of Wales, with a witticism of his own, expressed a desire to meet the young wit who was the toast of society – 'I do not know Oscar Wilde, and not to know him is not to be known.' Willie, having eschewed the law as a career, had taken a sidestep into journalism, and many of the positive accounts in the gossip columns of Oscar's London exploits came from his brother's pen. Oscar was becoming famous, although he had not yet produced any work worthy of note.

It is better to have a permanent income than to be fascinating.

In the background, however, he was writing. In 1880 he finished his first play, *Vera: Or the Nihilists*. It was loosely based on an actual event in Russia in 1880 but was riddled with historical inaccuracies and anomalies. Oscar had it printed privately and he sent copies to famous literary names for review. He was an excellent self-publicist – throughout his career he would send copies of his works to the literati of the day with requests for positive comments. He sent a copy of *Vera* to the Lord Chamberlain with the note that he was

> … working on dramatic art because it's the democratic art, and I want fame, so any suggestion, any helpful advice, your experience and very brilliant critical powers can give me I shall thank you very much for.

Despite his efforts to promote the play, it met with little enthusiasm from London's theatrical management.

By this time, Frank Miles had moved house, and Oscar had moved with him. They were now in Chelsea, in a house in Tite Street, arbitrarily renamed 'Keats House' by Oscar. Chelsea, although not as fashionable as it is today, was the base for the

Fashion is what one wears oneself. What is unfashionable is what other people wear.

> There is always more brass than brains in an aristocracy.

Aesthetic movement, whose philosophy permeated all aspects of the lives of its adherents. Not alone did they believe in 'art for art's sake', they thought that life itself should imitate art. Everything, from clothing to house furnishings, should be chosen for aesthetic value. Edward Godwin, who had refurbished the painter James McNeill Whistler's studio near Tite Street in the Aesthetic style (it was known as The White House), was chosen to redesign Keats House. Whistler and Oscar became friends, and conducted their friendship loudly and in public. Aesthetes were considered to be effete and lacking masculinity, and Whistler and Oscar were constantly lampooned by the satirists of the day. Oscar appeared in satirical cartoons as Oscuro Wildgoose and Ossian Wilderness, but he didn't react, doubtless aware that there is no such thing as bad publicity.

Oscar used his rooms in Keats House as the backdrop for his constantly growing collection of beautiful things. The Aesthetic makeover of the house showcased them perfectly. The popular gatherings at Salisbury Street and Keats House were referred to by Oscar and Miles as 'Tea and Beauties'. They were heavily attended by bored young women who had been presented at Court and were on the marriage round. Oscar and his friends called them the 'Professional Beauties', or PBs, and he delighted them with his witty conversation. Through Frank Miles, who was drawing her likeness, Oscar met Lillie Langtry, mistress of the Prince of Wales, and popularly known as the 'Jersey Lily' (she came from the Channel Islands). He began to be seen about town with her and frequently presented her with lilies, emblematic of purity, which had by now become his trademark. Langtry provided a detailed description of Oscar's dress at that time. In an era when men dressed with dark and sombre uniformity Oscar wore 'light-coloured trousers, a black frock coat, brightly coloured waistcoats with a white silk cravat held with an amethyst pin and always carrying lavender gloves.'

Oscar wrote a long poem for Langtry entitled 'The New Helen', in which he compared her to Helen of Troy. The final verse reads:

> *Lily of love, pure and inviolate!*
> *Tower of ivory! red rose of fire!*
> *Thou hast come down our darkness to illume:*
> *For we, close-caught in the wide nets of Fate,*
> *Wearied with waiting for the World's Desire,*
> *Aimlessly wandered in the house of gloom,*
> *Aimlessly sought some slumberous anodyne*
> *For wasted lives, for lingering wretchedness,*
> *Till we beheld thy re-arisen shrine,*
> *And the white glory of thy loveliness.*

In May 1879 Oscar became acquainted with the great French actress Sarah Bernhardt, meeting her on her arrival in England at Folkestone and throwing armfuls of lilies at her feet, a flamboyant gesture that was guaranteed to get the attention of the press. Bernhardt, always open to dramatic expressions of adoration, was won over, and she became a frequent visitor to Keats House. She, too, was immortalised by Oscar, in 'Phèdre':

How vain and dull this common world must seem
To such a One as thou, who should'st have talked
At Florence with Mirandola, or walked
Through the cool olives of the Academe:
Thou should'st have gathered reeds from a green stream
For Goat-foot Pan's shrill piping, and have played
With the white girls in that Phaeacian glade
Where grave Odysseus wakened from his dream.
Ah! surely once some urn of Attic clay
Held thy wan dust, and thou hast come again
Back to this common world so dull and vain,
For thou wert weary of the sunless day,
The heavy fields of scentless asphodel,
The loveless lips with which men kiss in Hell.

In 1881 Gilbert and Sullivan's comic operetta, *Patience*, a farcical attack on the Aesthetic movement, opened in London. Its protagonist, a humourless character called Bunthorne, was clearly modelled on Oscar, aping his style of dress, his mannerisms and his declamatory delivery, and poking fun at his fascination for young women. Audiences were amused by Bunthorne's outlandish statements, including the declaration that:

> Never speak disrespectfully of society. Only people who can't get into it do that.

It is the wail of the poet's heart on discovering that everything is commonplace, to … cling passionately to one another and think of faint lilies.

Once again, Oscar failed to react publicly to his lampooning – he was actually delighted with the notoriety that was attaching to him. Gilbert and Sullivan had, unwittingly, done him a service. Not only did *Patience* make Oscar one of the most talked about individuals in London, it would be his springboard to international fame.

In the meantime, Oscar had been working on another project – compiling a collection of his poetry, called, rather prosaically, *Poems*. Some of his poems had already been published in periodicals and he had additional unpublished verse that brought the total number of poems in the collection to about 60. The Newdigate prize-

Drawing of Wilde, 1882

winning poem, 'Ravenna', was not included. The poems, written during different periods of his life, sat alongside each other rather uneasily – possibly aware of the unevenness of the collection he asked the reader's indulgence in view of the fact that the poems were written during his childhood and adolescence. Oscar himself believed that the regretful sonnet 'Hélas!', written during his Oxford days, was the most characteristic poem in the collection:

To drift with every passion till my soul
Is a stringed lute upon which all winds can play,
Is it for this that I have given away
Mine ancient wisdom and austere control?
Methinks my life is a twice-written scroll
Scrawled over on some boyish holiday
With idle songs for pipe and virelay
Which do but mar the secret of the whole.
Surely there was a time I might have trod
The sunlit heights, and from life's dissonance
Struck one clear chord to reach the ears of God:
Is that time dead? lo! with a little rod
I did but touch the honey of romance –
And I must lose a soul's inheritance?

Some of the poems included in this volume, like 'Ballade de Marguerite', were chivalrously romantic in tone and expression, others, such as 'Easter Day' and 'San Miniato' were piously Christian, while yet others, exemplified by the throbbing verse of the long poem 'Charmides', were overtly sensual and likely to shock the sensibilities of the straitlaced Victorian public. Oscar paid the costs of publication, and his love of beautiful books manifested itself in the expensive production. The initial run of 250 copies was extravagantly produced on handmade paper with a parchment binding. It was usual for writers of the time to send copies of their publications to their entire circle of acquaintances and Oscar complied enthusiastically with tradition, sending copies of *Poems* to friends, academics, critics and writers, including Swinburne and Matthew Arnold. He wrote to Robert Browning, enclosing a copy:

> Will you accept from me the first copy of my poems – the only tribute I can offer you in return for the delight and the wonder which the strength and splendour of your work has given me from my boyhood.

The collection did not meet with critical success. One reviewer wrote: 'The poet is Wilde, but the poetry's tame.' The *Saturday Review* was scathing:

Mr Wilde's verses belong to a class which is the special terror of reviewers, the poetry which is neither good nor bad, which calls for neither praise nor ridicule. The author possesses cleverness, astonishing fluency, a rich and full vocabulary and nothing to say. Mr Wilde has read Messrs Tennyson, Swinburne, Arnold and Rossetti ... and he has paid them the compliment of copying their mannerisms very naively.

The Oxford Union asked for a copy, but returned it on the grounds that the poetry was both immoral and derivative. More devastatingly, on a practical and personal level, Frank Miles's father wrote to Frank and Oscar demanding that Oscar, who was obviously an unhealthy influence on Frank, move out of Keats House immediately. He wrote to Oscar:

[I]t is not because we do not believe you in character to be very different to what you suggest in your poetry, but because you do not see the risk we see in a published poem which makes all who read it say to themselves, 'this is outside the pale of poetry', it is licentious and may do great harm to any soul who reads it.

Frank was dependent on his father financially and had no option but to ask Oscar to leave. Furious at Frank's disloyalty, Oscar collected his things angrily and left the house, swearing never to speak to his friend again.

Oscar moved in with his mother and then repaired to some rooms at Charles Street, just off Grosvenor Square. They were not as salubrious as his former accommodation and were inadequate to the task of providing a backdrop to the beautiful things he had accumulated during the years he had spent as Miles's lodger. Life was not following Oscar's chosen trajectory – both *Vera* and his *Poems* were critical failures that would lead neither to fame nor to fortune. He had almost exhausted his inheritance and was living way beyond his means. And then, on 30 September 1881, he received a telegram from the impresario Richard D'Oyly Carte in New York. The message it conveyed was a life changer.

Gilbert and Sullivan's *Patience* had opened in New York in September 1881. American audiences, unfamiliar with the real-life character on whom Bunthorne was based, had no context for the libretto and were lukewarm in their reception. Sarah Bernhardt had suggested to D'Oyly Carte that a series of readings by Oscar Wilde might pique their interest. The American public had responded enthusiastically to a reading tour by Charles Dickens in 1866.

Oscar's reception of the proposal was favourable, especially as he hoped to be able to stage *Vera* in New York, with the actress Clara Morris taking the lead role (he was to be disappointed in that ambition), but planning the trip was slow, especially when it became clear that American audiences were now more interested in lectures than in readings. What would he lecture on?

In matters of grave importance, style, not sincerity, is the vital thing.

Detail from a cartoon in the US publication *The Judge*.

Beauty and aesthetics seemed an obvious choice and the idea of 'The English Renaissance', loosely based on Walter Pater's teachings, was formulated. While he had been quite prepared to give readings, Oscar felt unequal to the oratorical requirements of a lecture, so he took some elocution lessons to prepare himself for the task ahead. He planned his wardrobe carefully, and his commissioning of a long fur-trimmed green coat to cope with the rigours of the North American winter received full coverage in the British press. His lecture notes still unfinished, he embarked on the SS *Arizona* on 24 December 1881 and arrived in New York on 2 January 1882.

SS *Arizona*, the 'fastest steamer afloat'.

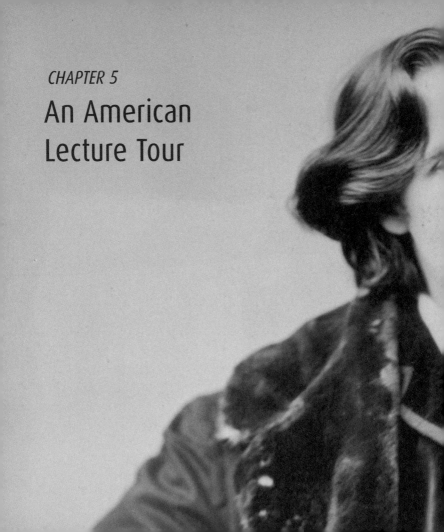

CHAPTER 5

An American
Lecture Tour

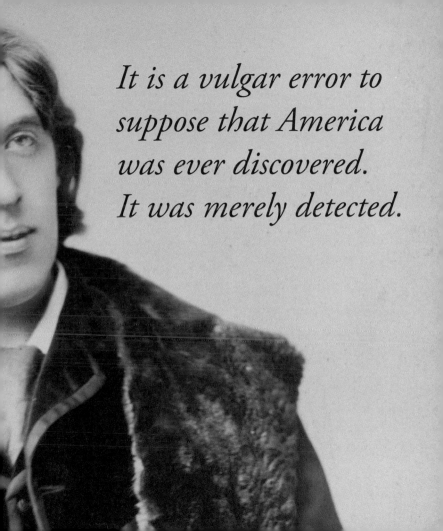

It is a vulgar error to suppose that America was ever discovered. It was merely detected.

O scar's tour had excited the interest of the US press, some of whom arrived at the ship on a small launch. Oscar, wearing his extravagant fur-trimmed coat, greeted them enthusiastically, and reports on his appearance and his impressions of the voyage appeared in the next day's papers. Once on dry land, Oscar was treated like royalty. He had hundreds of letters of introduction, and although he was supposed to be hiding himself away to finish writing his lecture, he attended the many receptions and parties that were given in his honour. Socially, he was making an impression, but he finally managed to step back from social circles to finish his lecture.

On 9 January he stood before a sell-out audience on the stage of Chickering Hall, dressed in knee breeches and silk stockings (his Masonic attire), frilled shirt cuffs under a purple coat lined with lilac, and shoes with large shiny buckles. His hair was long and parted in the middle. He had arrived on

America is the only country that went from barbarism to decadence without civilisation in between.

stage with a cloak slung casually over his shoulder. His lecture was polished. It dealt with beauty and life and the notion of art for art's sake, and asserted the importance of the English Renaissance, which he claimed was the equal of that of the Italian variety. He touched on his association with the lily, praising lilies and sunflowers as the blooms most adapted to the decorative arts. He finished his lecture with a rousing statement:

> We spend our days looking for the secret of Life. Well, the secret of Life is Art!

The audience was impressed, although some of them found the lecture dull. It was followed by a reception and an outing to a club. Oscar was delighted with the reaction to his lecture and wrote to a friend:

> I am sure you would have been pleased at my success! The hall had an audience

larger and more wonderful than even Dickens had ... Loving virtuous obscurity as much as I do, you can judge how much I dislike this lionizing ...

His next lecture was in Philadelphia, where he was invited to meet one of his literary heroes, Walt Whitman. Oscar introduced himself grandiloquently. 'I have come to you as to one with whom I have been acquainted almost since the cradle.' They had a cordial meeting, but Whitman later criticised Oscar

Letter of invitation from Walt Whitman to Oscar Wilde and a photographic portrait of Whitman.

for using verse as part of a literary performance. In the following three months he lectured in Washington DC, Baltimore, Upstate New York, Boston, Chicago and various Mid-West towns and cities, finishing up in California. On 23 January his mother, enthusiastic as always, wrote: 'I think your reception seems a triumph!'

His reception was not always favourable. The press could be disparaging and cutting, twisting his words and editing his epigrams, and he had soon tempered his welcoming attitude towards journalists. Some of their friendliness disappeared when faced with what they may have regarded as his arrogance. In the course of an interview with *The Omaha Herald*, he said

I'm a very ambitious young man. I want to do everything in the world. I cannot conceive of anything that I do not want to do. I want to write a great deal more poetry. I want to study painting more than I've been able to. I want to write a great many more plays, and I want to make this artistic movement the basis for a new civilisation.

The editor of the *New York Tribune* described Oscar as a

'pretentious fraud' and kept up a campaign against him throughout his year in the US. Oscar wondered aloud why it was that Americans were treated better in England than Englishmen were treated in America.

Nor did his encounters with the nation's literary heavyweights always go well. An introduction to the novelist Henry James was not a success. James found Oscar lightweight and lacking seriousness and reported to a friend that 'Hosscar Wilde is a fatuous fool … an unclean beast.' Some believe that James's antipathy towards Oscar was because he displayed the ambivalent sexuality that James himself kept well hidden from view. Oscar would later write that 'Mr James writes fiction as if it were a painful duty.'

However, press aside, Oscar was in great demand. He soon discovered that

> I am always astonishing myself. It is the only thing that makes life worth living.

his lecture on the English Renaissance was being reproduced almost verbatim by the press on the Eastern seaboard, and he realised that he would need to provide something new for his audiences. His second lecture was called 'The House Beautiful', a subject near to his heart for the opportunities it provided for the practical application of his Aesthetic principles. He first delivered it in Chicago in February, and then added a third lecture, 'The Decorative Arts', which put forward many of the tenets of the English Arts and Crafts movement, extolling the virtues of individually crafted items of furniture or decoration. It was during this lecture that he declared that 'Bad art is worse than no art.' As he became a more accomplished public speaker he tailored his lectures to his audiences, delivering commentary on various local landmarks from an Aesthetic perspective. Wherever he went he visited the local art gallery and art school, gave numerous interviews and attended receptions and dinners that were held in his honour.

Oscar had planned to end his tour in April, but favourable reviews of his appearances spread like wildfire and requests for bookings flooded in from all over the country. He stayed in the

> I have nothing to declare except my genius.

US until the end of the year, delivering a total of 140 lectures between January and October. The pace was hectic: 'Somewhere and sometime – I am not sure where or when', was the heading on one of his letters. He was addressed respectfully wherever he went in the US, reporting that 'When I went to Texas I was called "Captain", when I got to the centre of the country I was called "Colonel", and on arriving at the borders of Mexico, "General".'

However, it was not all lecturing – Oscar had enough hours of leisure to have an interesting time during his travels. In March he was brought to one of the silver mines in Leadville, Colorado, dressed in baggy trousers and a miner's hat for the occasion. Leadville was so high in the Rocky Mountains that he had altitude sickness, notwithstanding which he took the opportunity to inspect the mine in person. He went down in a bucket and was given a drill with which to open a new shaft, named in his honour. He was then invited by the miners to a supper, a source of amusement to him as it consisted solely of whiskey. He is said to have revelled in the miners' naked torsos. When asked later if he thought the miners were rough and ready, he revealed the common touch that was so characteristic of his encounters in later life, saying that they were 'Ready, but not rough. They were polished and refined compared with the people I met in larger cities farther East.'

In April he was brought to visit the penitentiary in Lincoln, Nebraska, where he was confirmed in a common prejudice of the time when he found that all the prisoners he met were 'mean looking, which consoled me, for I should hate to see a criminal with a noble face'. Later that month he was invited to tea at the studio of some young artists in San Francisco and found that it had been aesthetically decorated for the occasion.

Not all of his encounters with Americans were favourable. In July, he came face to face with racism in Atlanta, Georgia, when his black valet was not allowed to travel with him in a sleeping car. In New York in December, not long before he returned to England, he fell foul of an intricate gambling scam engineered by a notorious confidence trickster. When he complained to the police the press got wind of the event and the *New York Tribune* published a mocking verse:

And then, with the air of a guileless child,
Oh, that sweet bright smile and those eyes aflame,
He said, 'If you'll let me, dear Mr Wilde,
I'll show you a ravishing little game.'

As he crossed the US Oscar discovered that his Irishness was a favourable characteristic in some quarters where Irish Americans revered him as the son of Speranza Wilde. In St Paul, Minnesota, an Irish priest introduced him to his audience as the son of 'one of Ireland's noblest daughters – who in the troublous times of 1848 by the works of her pen and her noble example did much to keep the fire of patriotism burning brightly'. Oscar rose to the challenge of resurrecting that part of him that he had subdued since his Oxford days, describing the Irish race as the 'most aristocratic in Europe', and declaring his firm belief in Republicanism. He wrote a fourth lecture, entitled

'The Irish Poets of 1848', many of whom he had met during his childhood at his mother's Dublin salon. In September the *Freeman's Journal* reported that Oscar was

> So completely filling all America with his renown that the country is absolutely bursting … He has risen above every insult and condemnation and will return home filled with respect for his own capacity and justly proud of his own perseverance … He is rich by his own labour, and will be respected now in spite of the strange attire he assumes.

That Oscar had a sharp wit was apparent to anyone who encountered him, but it was tempered with an innate kindness, and he always took seriously the people who sent him samples of their work, even if he could find nothing of merit in them. During his tour of the US he wrote to an admirer, an

American girls are as clever at concealing their parents as English women are at concealing their past.

> I am not exactly pleased with the Atlantic, it is not so majestic as I expected.

aspiring poet, who had sent him her book of poems:

> I have read with much pleasure your charming little volume with all its sweet and simple joy in field and flower, its sympathetic touching of those chords of life which Death and Love make immortal for us.

Despite the success of his tour and the punishing lecture schedule, Oscar didn't lose sight of the fact that one of his reasons for coming to the US was to secure a production of his play *Vera*. On his return to New York in October he decided not to return to England immediately. He was suffering from malaria and didn't feel up to travelling, and he wanted to pin down the production of *Vera* and an as yet unwritten romantic melodrama set in 16th-century Italy, *The Duchess of Padua*. He also wanted to spend some time with Lillie Langtry who was due to arrive for a tour of the US with her own theatre company.

The actress arrived in New York on 23 October and Oscar went out to the SS *Arizona* meet her, bearing a huge armful of lilies. The *New York Times* recorded his appearance:

He was dressed as probably no grown man in the world was ever dressed before. His hat was of brown cloth not less than six inches high; his coat was of black velvet; his overcoat was of green cloth, heavily trimmed with fur; his trousers matched his hat; his tie was gaudy and his shirtfront very open, displaying a large expanse of manly chest. A pair of brown cloth gloves and several pimples on his chin completed his toilet. His flowing hair and the fur trimming of his coat were just of a shade, and they gave him the appearance of having his hair combed down one side of him to his heels and up the other side.

Oscar entertained Lillie Langtry during the week before her theatrical opening in New York. They visited the stylish photographer Napoleon Sarony, who photographed them both.

His portrait of Oscar is one of the most famous representations of the writer, and that of Langtry also became iconic.

His prolonged stay in New York meant that Oscar spent a lot of the money he had made, but he still had some left to take home with him. He had secured future productions of both *Vera* and *The Duchess of Padua*, with Marie Prescott and Mary Anderson in the respective title roles, and his US trip had enhanced his reputation on the other side of the Atlantic. On 18 September his mother wrote to him with her customary hyperbole:

> You are still the talk of London – the milkman has bought your picture! I think you will be mobbed when you come back by eager crowds and will be obliged to shelter in cabs.

Oscar left New York on 27 December 1882, having become a household name in the US. With the promise of production, his first priority would be to write *The Duchess of Padua*.

Oscar Wilde and Whistler, in a drawing by Phil May, 1894. The caption accompanying reads: 'That was an awfully [witty remark] good joke you made last/night. I wish I [had made it.] could say it was mine.'/'You will [underlined] my boy. You will [underlined].'

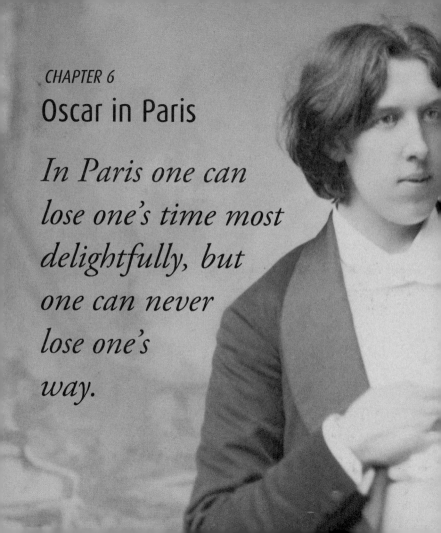

CHAPTER 6

Oscar in Paris

In Paris one can lose one's time most delightfully, but one can never lose one's way.

Oscar returned from the US with the remains of his earnings from his lecture tour and an advance on *The Duchess of Padua*. As one biographer pointed out, he was now famous without having produced anything of note – he may have been the first person who was famous for being famous. Although he was in demand with friends and family and dined out on tales of his experiences in the US, he soon became restless. Aestheticism had lost whatever momentum it had enjoyed, and Oscar was content to let it die a death, at least in public – his style of dress, while extreme by the standards of the times (who else in London wore a red suit?) lost its romantic foppishness – although he would always adhere to the principles of Aestheticism. Driven now by practicality, he knew that he needed to start work on his play, delivery of which he had promised for 1 March 1883, and he decided that Paris would be more conducive to writing than London was proving to be.

Why Paris? He had been there twice before and he spoke French fluently. He loved the city and regarded it as excitingly experimental in the cultural sphere. He arrived there at the end of January and established himself in a suite in the Hotel Voltaire on the Left Bank, where he had stayed with his mother on an earlier visit. Armed with the letters of introduction he had been given before his departure, he made a point of calling on the literary giants of Paris, including Victor Hugo, Paul Verlaine and the diarist Edmond de Goncourt. As was so often the case, Oscar's high expectations were not realised. Hugo slept through most of their meeting and Verlaine struck Oscar as shabby.

Between them Hugo and Shakespeare have exhausted every subject. Originality is no longer possible – even in sin. So there are no real emotions left – only extraordinary adjectives.

Oscar was now in the process of reinventing himself, setting aside the louche and indolent facade that he had constructed and turning towards modernism. This did not mean that he was turning his back on the principles of Aestheticism, merely adapting them to the cleaner, sharper times of the final decades of the 19th century. His clothing became, if not conventional, at least less unconventional – while in Paris he dressed like a Frenchman, with some embellishments, such as fancy linings, and he still wore the fur-trimmed coat that he had had made for his trip to the US. Inspired by a bust in the Louvre he had his hair cut short in the style of a Roman emperor so that it curled elegantly around his face.

At that time, the modern fashion for impressionism prevailed in contemporary French literature as it did in the art galleries and Oscar was greatly attracted by it. He became familiar with the works of the Impressionist painters, particularly Monet, Degas and Pissarro (he met Degas and Pissarro) and read many of the latest literary works. France was less restricted by censorship than England and hitherto unvoiced ideas were getting a public airing, including a discussion of homosexuality, which would have been beyond the Pale in London.

Although he was enjoying a busy social life in the evenings, attending parties, dining out and going to the theatre, Oscar's days were spent working at a desk in the sitting-room of his hotel suite. The punctual delivery of *The Duchess of Padua* required a punishing pace of work. He wrote in a white dressing gown, covering sheet after sheet of expensive paper with his large scrawl. Despite his best efforts, the manuscript of the play was delivered two weeks late. However, his usual confidence manifested itself in his letter to Mary Anderson, in which he highlighted for her the wonderful acting opportunity he was giving her:

> I have no hesitation in saying that it is the masterpiece of all my literary work, the *chef d'oeuvre* of my youth.

The value of an idea has nothing whatsoever to do with the sincerity of the man who expresses it.

I like men who have a future and women who have a past.

The *chef d'oeuvre* was melodramatic and romantic: Guido, the son of the murdered Duke of Padua, swears to kill his father's murderer, who is the current Duke. The Duchess is in love with Guido and, believing that he wants to murder her husband to set her free, kills the Duke herself. Guido is horrified and the Duchess points to him as the murderer, although she later regrets this. Condemned to death, Guido refuses to let her take the blame.

A deafening silence greeted the delivery of the manuscript. When he still hadn't heard anything at the end of April, Oscar sent Mary Anderson a telegram and received one by return. Her response to his play was an emphatic 'No', embellished in a letter she sent a few days later.

Neither of us can afford failure now, and your Duchess in my hands would not succeed, as

the part does not fit me. My admiration of your ability is
as great as ever.

Oscar was not unduly rattled by this unexpected turn of
events. He still had the forthcoming US production of *Vera*,
starring Marie Prescott, to look forward to. Prescott was
pleased with some minor revisions of the play that she had
asked him for, and she now wrote to him asking him to come
to the final rehearsal on 18 August.

The biggest dent produced by the rejection of his
manuscript seems to have been not to his pride, but to his
wallet. His funds were almost exhausted as he had been living
in his usual extravagant and generous fashion and he had
been counting on his take of the eventual box office receipts.
He had been dining out very well every evening, funded by
the advance he had received for the play – 'dining with the
Duchess', as he put it, to his chief dining companion, an
aspiring young English writer called Robert Sherard, a great
grandson of William Wordsworth.

After a rocky start to their acquaintance, Sherard was
prepared to idolise Oscar and their friendship would last

> To be natural is such a very difficult pose to keep up.

20 years (Sherard, who wrote a number of biographies of Oscar, proved to be one of his most loyal friends). Although Sherard later admitted to Oscar that his first impression of him was that he was a fraud, he remembered that first encounter rather differently in *The Real Oscar Wilde*, published in 1915:

> On that first night in Paris, [Wilde] appeared to me one of the most wonderful beings that I had ever met.

Whatever the truth of the matter, by the end of that first evening (they were dining at a friend's house) Sherard had been won over by Oscar's erudite wit and charm and Oscar sought him out to invite him to dine with him the following evening. Initially Sherard addressed him as Wilde, following the convention of the time, but Oscar responded, 'You mustn't call me Wilde. If I

Robert Sherard

> I think that generosity is the essence of friendship.

am your friend, my name to you is Oscar. If we are only strangers, I am Mr Wilde.' It was Oscar's habit to use people's given names, a leap of familiarity in the formal Victorian age.

Oscar and Sherard began to spend a lot of time in each other's company and soon they were seeing each other every day. Although Sherard was Oscar's 'type' – young (21), fair, masculine and, by some accounts, handsome – he never had any sense that his new friend was interested in him sexually, although Oscar did once kiss him on the lips, socially. They spoke of literature, and whether Sherard, who was considering it, should get married (Oscar advised him not to, on the grounds that wives' unfaithfulness was almost universal). Oscar, consciously or unconsciously, was using Sherard as a sounding board, shaping

Robert Sherard

and refining the witticisms that would appear in his later plays. Sherard could be counted on to make notes of Oscar's better aphorisms.

Oscar spent many of his evenings at the theatre, probably trying to think of a way to have at least one of his plays staged in Paris, but his hopes were dashed when he went to the Vaudeville Theatre with Sherard to see Sarah Bernhardt in a play called *Fédora*, bearing a huge armful of wallflowers which he presented to the actress between acts. He must have felt thwarted when he realised, as the play unfolded on stage, that its substance was remarkably similar to that of his *Vera* script. *The Duchess of Padua*, written in blank verse, was untranslatable as a dramatic work.

While in Paris Wilde worked hard and played equally hard. He himself recognised

I like looking at geniuses, and listening to beautiful people.

The worst thing you can do for a person of genius is to help him: that way lies his destruction. I have had many devoted helpers – and you see the result.

that it had been a productive time, 'putting black upon white, black upon white'. He even started to work again on his poem 'The Sphinx', started during his 1874 visit to Paris with his mother. He scoured dictionaries for rhyming words that would fit his verse and enlisted Sherard's help in the task. However, by the middle of May his money had run out and Sherard had gone to London. Oscar had no real reason to stay in Paris, so he returned to his mother's house at Grosvenor Square.

'The Sphinx', by Oscar Wilde, with decorations by Charles Ricketts (1894).

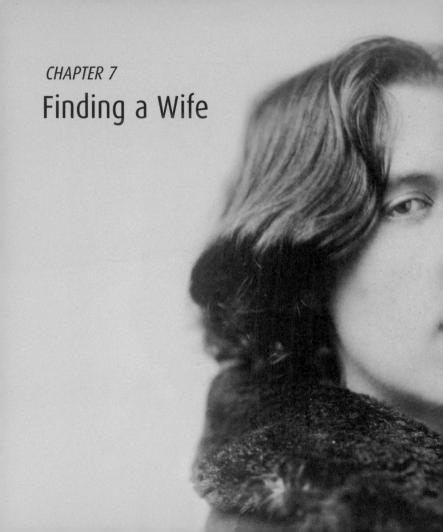

Finding a Wife

*If we men married
the women we deserve
we should have a very
bad time of it.*

On his return to London Oscar decided to stay with his mother while he marshalled himself to do something about repairing the state of his finances. He wrote to his friend Steele Mackaye, asking for the repayment of a loan: 'I have had a great many expenses over here, and bills of my Oxford days (black and white spectres of dead dissipations!) have crowded on me as thick as quails in the desert, and not as nice.' Habitually generous, Oscar must have found it difficult to call in his loan to a friend.

Meanwhile, money matters aside, he was delighted to be back in London, writing to Sherard of 'the splendid swirl and whirl of life in London'. 'I am hard at work being idle,' he added, ' … late midnights and famishing morrows follow one another … However, society must be amazed, and my Neronian coiffure has amazed it.' On 23 May his new hairstyle was lampooned in the *World*:

Our Oscar is with us again, but, O,
He is changed who was once so fair!
Has the iron gone into his soul? O no!
It has only gone over his hair.

Oscar was more determined than ever to make his mark, and he decided to organise a series of public lectures – one on his impressions of the US and the other on a subject he had lectured on during his tour, 'The House Beautiful'.

Lady Wilde was still championing her own solution to the parlous state of Oscar's finances, encouraging both of her sons to get themselves engaged to heiresses. She had even suggested to Oscar that 'you must bring home the American bride', so it must have been galling that Oscar had spent a whole year in the US without attaching himself to a rich American. Oscar knew that he would have to marry, if only to

Once a week is quite enough to propose to anyone, and it should always be done in a manner that attracts some attention.

> Nothing spoils a romance as much as a sense of humour in the woman – or the want of it in the man.

quell the rumours that were circulating about his sexuality. But he was a romantic – he had lost Florence Balcombe, and his proposal to Charlotte Montefiore, sister of one of Oscar's Oxford contemporaries, had been refused in 1880 or 1881. If he was devastated, it didn't affect his wit – he wrote to Charlotte on the evening of her refusal, 'I am so sorry about your decision. With your money and my brain we could have gone far.'

In May 1881, Oscar was making a social call with his mother when he was introduced to Constance Lloyd at her grandparents' house in London. Her brother Otho had been slightly acquainted with him at Oxford. Constance was shy and a bit awkward in company, but Oscar quickly put her at her ease. She wrote to Otho, 'I can't help liking him, because when he's talking

Constance Lloyd by Louis William Desanges, 1882

110

to me alone he's never a bit affected, and speaks naturally, excepting that he uses better language than most people.' Oscar was soon a frequent visitor. Nothing was said or promised, but while Oscar was away in the US and Paris, Constance attended art school and began to dress in the Aesthetic fashion, which outlawed corsetry, hoops and other restricting garments. She attended pottery classes and started a collection of blue and white china, *de rigueur* in Aesthetic circles.

Tall, beautiful, clever and accomplished, Constance was three years younger than Oscar. In stark contrast to Oscar's happy childhood with indulgent and engaged parents, hers had been miserable. Her parents were cold and distant, and when her father died during her adolescence, her mother became both verbally and physically abusive of her, denigrating her in public and sometime behaving violently in private. When her mother remarried, Constance went to live with her grandparents and it was at their home that Oscar met her. As children, she and her brother had spent time at their grandmother's house in Ely Place in Dublin, not far from the Wilde's home on Merrion Square. The families moved in the same circles, so it is likely that the

I have always been of the opinion that a man who desires to get married should know either everything or nothing.

Lloyd children met the Wilde boys during their visits to Dublin.

By any standard, Constance was well educated, an accomplished pianist, painter and needleworker and very well read. Like Oscar, she spoke French fluently, and she was able to read Dante in Italian. She had been tutored by a governess and also took university-standard courses at women's colleges (women could not earn degrees at that time). In so many respects, she was the perfect woman for Oscar.

Oscar was certainly attracted to Constance. He addressed her by her first name, a sure sign of familiarity in Victorian social circles, although it was something of a habit with Oscar to address his friends by their given names. They went to art exhibitions together and he took her to a performance of *Othello* at the Lyceum, with

Constance Lloyd before her marriage to Oscar.

Ellen Terry playing Desdemona. Constance took to waiting in at home in the hope that he might call and soon they were seeing each other almost every day. By the end of the year Constance was completely infatuated, and was not ashamed to wear her heart on her sleeve.

In January Oscar left England for his lecture tour of the US, believing that he would be returning to London in April. The extension of his tour to the end of the year must have been difficult for Constance, but it is likely that they were writing to each other frequently. In September the gossip column in the *Freeman's Journal* carried a report that must have been heart-stopping for her:

> [T]he great aim of his life is about to be accomplished (so folks declare) by a rich and laudable marriage with the daughter of the great American actress Julia Ward Howe. Miss Maud Howe was one of the beauties of the London season some three years ago, and obtained the honour of especial notice by one of the gallant sons of royalty.

The report had no foundation, but it was covered sufficiently widely that Oscar asked his mother to quell the rumours in

London. He arrived back in London, unencumbered by fiancée or wife, at the beginning of 1883. He had hardly drawn breath, however, before he set off on his travels again, this time to Paris, to write *The Duchess of Padua*. On his return, he and Constance picked up where they had left off and they saw as much of each other as they could. However, Oscar had a date with *Vera* in New York in August, and he left London in July so that he could fit in a series of lectures in Margate, Ramsgate, Southampton, Brighton and Southport. He then went to Liverpool, where he embarked for New York on 2 August. *Vera* was a flop and closed after a week. Oscar was back in London by October. He had a brief encounter with Constance at his mother's salon, but then her grandfather fell gravely ill and she went to Dublin in early November to stay with her maternal grandmother.

I am not in favour of long engagements. They give people the opportunity of finding out each other's character before marriage, which I think is never advisable.

Constance wrote to Oscar from Dublin, commiserating with him on the failure of his play, and inviting him to visit when he came to the city for a series of lectures. He arrived in Dublin on 21 November and set himself up in the Shelbourne Hotel on St Stephen's Green. He went to visit Constance that evening, and the following evening she and her family went to his 'House Beautiful' lecture in the Gaiety Theatre. Oscar and Constance's romance proceeded apace and just a week later, she was writing to her brother Otho: 'Prepare yourself for an astounding piece of news! I am engaged to Oscar Wilde and perfectly and insanely happy.'

Oscar gave Constance a diamond and pearl ring that he had designed himself, then left Dublin to allow her to win her family over to the idea of their marriage. He wrote to her every day and she responded passionately.

My own Darling Oscar

I have just got your letter and your letters always make me mad for joy and yet more mad to see you and feel once again that you are mine and that it is not a dream but a living

Constance Wilde, c.1884

> One should always be in love. That is the reason one should never marry.

reality that you love me … I can only dream of you all day long and it seems as if everyone I meet must know my secret and see in my face how I love you, my own love.

Lady Wilde had encouraged and facilitated the match and Constance's family gradually grew used to the idea, but her grandfather insisted on being satisfied as to Oscar's prospects before he would give his consent to the marriage. Oscar was candid about his debts, and the old man set up a small trust fund for Constance so that the couple could marry sooner rather than later. It was enough to support them, but not enough that Oscar would face accusations of gold digging.

They could now begin to plan their wedding, but Oscar wanted to prove himself to Constance's grandfather as a reliable breadwinner, and he committed himself to a series of lectures that would keep him busy for about two years. Constance pined during the absences that this entailed. 'I cannot fight against my dread of your going away,' she wrote. 'Do believe that I love you most passionately with all the strength of my heart and mind: anything that you asked me to do, I would, in order to convince you and make you happy.'

There has long been speculation about whether Constance was aware of Oscar's homosexual tendencies. It is unlikely. In Victorian Britain sexuality was not a subject that was discussed in society drawing rooms or even behind closed doors, and although *Punch* had jeered at Oscar's 'Mary-Ann' tendencies, much of the gossip related to the way he dressed and carried himself. As far as anyone knew,

A man can be happy with any woman as long as he does not love her.

The worst of having a romance of any kind is that it leaves one so unromantic.

the closest he had come to an expression of homosexuality was in his verse. All of his romantic and sexual attachments thus far had been with women. He had had a couple of love attachments with young women and he had employed the services of female prostitutes in Oxford and Paris. When he became engaged to Constance he wrote to Lillie Langtry:

> I am going to be married to a beautiful girl called Constance Lloyd, a grave, slight, violet-eyed Artemis, with great coils of heavy brown hair which make her flower-like head droop like a flower, and wonderful ivory hands which draw music from the piano so sweet that the birds stop singing to listen to her … I am hard at work lecturing and getting quite rich, tho' it is horrid being so much away from her.

The engagement was announced publicly in December and Constance immediately became the focus of attention. Unused to being in the public eye, she was overwhelmed by the flood of cards and messages of congratulation that she received. Lillie Langtry expressed herself unsurprised by the news, 'as I knew that he had for some time admired the girl'.

The wedding took place at 2.30 pm on 29 May 1884 at St James's Church, Sussex Gardens. Crowds of Oscar's fans were waiting outside the church to see Constance arrive in the dress she had designed herself. There had been rumours that it was saffron-coloured, following the tradition of the ancient Greeks, but it was actually ivory with a delicate tint of yellow. In accordance with Aesthetic style requirements it had a plain bodice, puffed

If one really loves a woman, all other women in the world become absolutely meaningless to one.

Men always want to be a woman's first love. That is their clumsy vanity. Women have a more subtle instinct about things. What they like is to be a man's last romance.

sleeves and no bustle. Her silk veil was embroidered with pearls and she had a silver girdle around her waist. Her bouquet was of lilies. Oscar's apparel may have disappointed his fans – he was wearing an ordinary frock coat.

Constance had six bridesmaids, two wearing terracotta coloured dresses and the other four dressed in pale blue with gold figuring. They had high straw hats trimmed with feathers and silk. Amber necklaces and bouquets of water lilies finished the spectacle. Oscar's best man was Willie. There was a brief reception at Constance's grandfather's house at Lancaster Gate, and then the newlyweds boarded the 4.30 from Charing Cross en route to their honeymoon in Paris.

Constance Wilde, c.1887.

CHAPTER 8

Marriage and Family

The proper basis for marriage is mutual misunderstanding.

In Paris the honeymooning Wildes took a suite of rooms in a modest hotel on the rue de Rivoli with a view of the Tuileries Gardens. They used it as a base from which to entertain and be entertained. They visited art galleries and went to the theatre to see Sarah Bernhardt play Lady Macbeth. They gave dinners and were invited to lunches, teas and dinners. Oscar was attentive to Constance, showering her with flowers and love tokens at every opportunity.

Sherard was also back in Paris and Oscar spent a good deal of time with him, wandering the streets in a reprise of his bachelor days, taking in the sights and the seedier clubs that he had previously felt drawn to. Despite his declarations of adoration, Oscar felt the need to do things without Constance. Perhaps he was finding it difficult to adjust to the married state – like most Victorian couples they didn't really know each other very well. Soon Oscar was joking that marriage should be contracted for seven years, with a right of renewal by each party.

Constance thought a mere 12 months should be the contracted period.

With her commitment to the ideals of Aestheticism, Constance was in many ways the ideal partner for Oscar. On her honeymoon she unveiled a wardrobe that put those ideals into practice. The *Lady's Pictorial* reported that

> Mrs Oscar Wilde, in her large white plumed hats, in her long dust cloaks of creamy alpaca richly trimmed with ruches of coffee coloured lace, in her fresh and somewhat quaintly-made gowns of white muslin, usually relieved by touches of golden ribbon … is declared to be 'charmante' and to be dressed with absolute good taste.

When the celebrity couple returned to London after their honeymoon, people

Men marry because they are tired; women because they are curious; both are disappointed.

in Britain couldn't get enough of them and crowds gathered whenever they were seen in public. Constance's original way of dressing was approved by the bohemian Arts and Crafts fraternity, but in other quarters she was regarded as eccentric. The couple was considered even more eccentric on the occasions when Constance and Oscar wore matching outfits. However, those efforts at sartorial coordination were infrequent and soon Oscar had cast aside his own eccentric style and was dressing conventionally, albeit with original touches of flamboyance.

In October 1884, Oscar gave a lecture in Ealing on the subject of dress. He extolled the superiority of the medieval robes that were replaced after 1066 by more contrived French fashions. He was in favour of what he called 'rational' dress for women, promoting loose clothing and flat shoes – this was a

Ball gown designed by Jacques Doucet, 1898–1900, with characteristics of the Aesthetic dress movement: simple in design, 'yet extravagant by the choice of materials used'.

radical departure from the contrived and restricting fashions of the late Victorian era. However, it was not long before the public was won over – rational dress was branded 'hygienic', meaning healthy, and the Prince of Wales gave it his seal of approval.

Another of Oscar's lectures, 'The House Beautiful', provided the template for the newly-weds' decoration of the house at 16 Tite Street, Chelsea, leased by Oscar in the year of their marriage. It was new house, built over four floors and although it retained its conventional exterior throughout their occupation, Oscar and Constance decided to have the interior completely redesigned in the Aesthetic style by the fashionable architect of the day, Edward Godwin. There was no sign of the dark, heavy style of decoration that was fashionable in the late Victorian era. Instead the interiors were plain and simple, with the walls painted white or in strong colours instead of being covered with flocked wallpaper. With the exception of Oscar's more conventionally furnished library, the decor was plain and simple. The floor coverings were pale and delicately patterned. Internal doors were replaced by curtains, and the furniture was small and light. The decorative style provided the perfect background for a display of paintings and *objets d'art* – one of Oscar's new lectures was entitled 'The Value of Art in Modern Life' and his house reflected his opinions on the subject. Victorians liked to display their wealth, but the Wilde home was more about good taste and refinement than ostentation. It was not long before it became known as the 'House Beautiful'.

It was some time before Oscar and Constance could move in – they had hoped to move in after their honeymoon, but Godwin was a slow and meticulous worker and the house wasn't ready for them until January 1885. It had been an expensive project, and Oscar's lecture fees disappeared as soon as he had earned them. However, Constance's grandfather had died a few months after their marriage, leaving her an annual income of £900 – not riches, but a sizeable income.

Number 16 Tite Street would be Oscar's only permanent home. Three rooms were designated for his exclusive use – his bedroom, library and smoking room. Above the entrance to the library there was a colourful, gilded inscription from Oscar's poem, 'The Garden of Eros':

Oscar's house at 34 Tite Street, formerly number 16, as it appeared in the 1880s and today.

Spirit of Beauty! tarry still awhile,
They are not dead, thine ancient votaries,
Some few there are to whom thy radian smile
Is better than a thousand victories.

The house was the perfect setting for entertaining the literati and intelligentsia of bohemian London and Oscar and Constance's twice-monthly 'at homes' soon became legendary. The house was also a perfect family home, and on 5 June 1885, Cyril arrived, after a birth described by Oscar as easy. He had been indulgent and supportive of Constance during her pregnancy and now he was a delighted father – he described Cyril as an 'amazing' and 'wonderful' child. In June 1996, Oscar wrote a poem to Constance.

I can write no stately poem
As a prelude to my lay
From a poet to a poem –
This is all I say.
Yet if of these fallen petals
One to you seems fair,
Love will waft it, till it settles
On your hair.
And when wind and winter harden
All the loveless land,
It will whisper of the garden,
You will understand

Constance and Cyril.

In married
life three is
company and
two is none.

The amount of women in London who flirt with their own husbands is perfectly scandalous. It looks so bad. It is simply washing one's clean linen in public.

However, by the time their second child, another son, was born in November 1886, Oscar's passion for his wife had diminished. During Constance's second pregnancy Oscar had buoyed himself up with the idea that the baby would be a girl. He and Constance had decided to call her Isola after Oscar's dead sister. Instead it was another boy, Vyvyan, and this second son was not as robust as his older brother. The disappointment of another son must have been great, as the baby's birth wasn't registered for several weeks, and neither parent was certain of the date of his birth. Although Constance and Oscar loved both their sons – unlike most Victorian middle-class parents they both spent a lot of time with them – there is no doubt that Cyril was their favourite. After his second encounter with morning sickness and the other physical manifestations of pregnancy,

Oscar no longer found his wife sexually alluring. Her boyish figure had been overtaken by womanly curves, and Oscar's earlier feelings for her had been replaced by an affection that he described as a 'curious mixture of ardour and indifference'.

Although Oscar always claimed to hanker after domesticity, the dull reality of married life seems to have caused it to lose its appeal for him. He loved Constance and his boys, but he had always enjoyed the company of young men. In 1887 a 17-year-old Canadian, Robert (Robbie) Ross, the son of an acquaintance of Constance, moved into Tite Street to live with Oscar and Constance as a paying guest while he crammed for the Cambridge entrance exam. He was clever and engaging and was already a practising homosexual. He accompanied the Wildes to the theatre,

There's nothing in the world like the devotion of a married woman. It's a thing no married man knows anything about.

lectures and art exhibitions and very soon he had become Oscar's first homosexual lover. Historically, it was a bad time for Oscar to acknowledge his sexuality – although sodomy had been outlawed for centuries, it wasn't until 1885, when a piece of legislation known as the Labouchère Amendment was passed, that other sexual relations between men, described as acts of 'gross indecency', became unlawful. Several male brothels were closed down. Ironically, Henry du Pré Labouchère was a great admirer of Oscar and his work – he had introduced his devastating amendment to the Criminal Law Amendment Act in an attempt to protect young boys who were working as prostitutes. Oscar's ill-timed entrance into the world of homosexual activity put him at grave risk of prosecution. Ross, who was openly homosexual, was known to the police, but by the time he had departed the household for Cambridge he and Oscar remained undetected.

Whatever Oscar's feelings about marriage and despite his involvement with Ross, he was a devoted family man. He had come to the realisation that his lectures took him away from home too frequently and that the income they produced was inadequate and unreliable. He was still a spendthrift, and any money he received slipped through his fingers too easily. He began to look for permanent employment in order to support his family adequately. An attempt to become a school inspector came to nothing. However, after three years of constant lecture tours he turned his attention to journalism, making regular contributions to the *Dramatic Review* and the *Pall Mall Gazette*. Reviewing was an activity he enjoyed – he would elevate it to an art form in his essay 'The Critic as Artist', published in 1891. In spring 1887 he was approached by London publishers Cassell & Co., who were starting up a new magazine for women, *The Lady's World: A Magazine of Fashion and Society*. Oscar's success with his lectures on interior design and rational dress, when looked at in conjunction with his famously fashionable

> In married life affection comes when people thoroughly dislike each other.

The one charm of marriage is that it makes a life of deception absolutely necessary for both parties.

wife, made him the ideal candidate for the editorship of the magazine. His response to the job offer shows that he thought himself equal to the challenge of contributing something different to the women's magazine market.

> It seems to me that at present it is too feminine, and not sufficiently womanly … the field of mere millinery and trimmings, is to some extent already occupied by such papers as the *Queen* and *Lady's Pictorial* … we should take a wider range, as well as a high standpoint, and deal not merely with what women wear, but with what they think, and what they feel.

Oscar became editor of the new magazine in May 1887 and he began soliciting articles from his wide acquaintance of literary women, many of whom were regulars at the Tite Street 'at homes'. Soon, following his own advice in his letter to the publishers, he had changed the focus of the magazine – he renamed it *Women's World* – and widened its scope to provide a forum for women's opinions on a wide range of subjects, including art and literature. Constance collaborated with him and contributed several articles, as did his mother, but circulation of the magazine dwindled and Oscar resigned his editorship in 1889.

In the meantime, perhaps encouraged by a successful endeavour of his wife's, that of publishing her tales for children, Oscar decided to publish his own collection of children's stories. His previous foray into fiction had been in 1887, when his short stories 'Lord Arthur Savile's Crime' and 'The Canterville Ghost', both with a

No man should have a secret from his wife – she invariably finds it out.

Christmas Eve.

fashionably occult theme, were published in instalments in the *Court and Society Review*.

The Happy Prince and Other Tales, published in 1888, was something completely different. Oscar had been immersed in Irish legends as a child and he later related them to spellbound audiences at fashionable gatherings in London and Paris. The stories are poignant and beautiful – when Oscar told the story of 'The Selfish Giant' to his children he wept. When they asked him why, he told them that beautiful things made him cry.

Oscar said that he had written these many-layered, multi-levelled stories as 'studies in prose … meant partly for children and partly for those who have kept the childlike faculties of wonder and joy'. When the collection was published Oscar sent a copy to Prime Minister Gladstone, a

The Happy Prince, 1888.

Illustration from *A Long Time Ago*, written by Constance Wilde *et al.*

English-women conceal their feelings till after they are married. They show them then.

well-known book lover. The accompanying note was uncharacteristically modest: 'It is only a collection of short stories, and it is really meant for children … '. This, however, was one occasion where he need not have played down his achievement. The critics and the public loved the stories, which eschewed the typical moral message of traditional fairy tales. The *Irish Times* described the collection as 'one of the happiest works which Mr Oscar Wilde has ever produced'. Publication of the collection marked the real beginning of Oscar's literary success.

Cover of *The Happy Prince and Other Tales* by Oscar Wilde, illustrated by Walter Crane.

THE HAPPY PRINCE
AND OTHER TALES BY
OSCAR WILDE
ILLUSTRATED BY
WALTER CRANE
& JACOMB
HOOD
1888

CHAPTER 9

The Picture of Dorian Gray

There is no such thing as an immoral book.
Books are well written or badly written. That is all.

Shortly after becoming acquainted with Robbie Ross, Oscar began thinking about writing another work of fiction. A short story entitled 'The Portrait of Mr W. H.' was finished in 1887, although it wasn't published until 1889. The 'W. H.' of the story is one of the boy actors who played female roles in Shakespeare's plays, as was the custom in the 16th century. The story was based on the premise that William Shakespeare was attracted to young men. Most of Oscar's friends to whom he showed the manuscript advised against seeking publication, on the grounds that it would corrupt public morals. Robbie Ross had inspired him to write the story of the married writer with two children, who becomes fascinated by a beautiful boy, and he encouraged him to have it published. The *Fortnightly Review* rejected it, but an edited version appeared in *Blackwood's Magazine* in July 1889. It received very little notice, although there was enough for people to start gossiping about Oscar. In view of Oscar's later liaisons, his description of the portrait of Shakespeare's putative love object is revealing.

> He seemed about seventeen years of age, and was of quite extraordinary personal beauty, though evidently somewhat effeminate. Indeed, had it not been for the dress and the closely cropped hair, one would have said that the face, with its dreamy wistful eyes, and its delicate scarlet lips, was the face of a girl.

The idea of a portrait freezing a moment of youthful, ephemeral beauty inspired Oscar's next work and his only novel, *The Picture of Dorian Gray*. Witty and highly readable, the novel sold out when it was published in the July 1890 issue of the US

The value of an idea has nothing whatsoever to do with the sincerity of the man who expresses it.

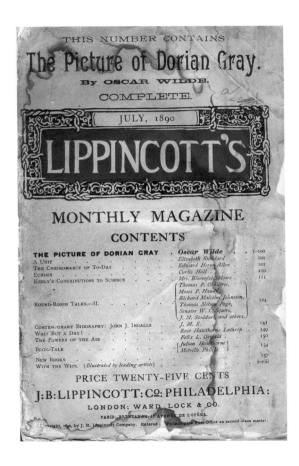

magazine, *Lippincott's Monthly*. A slightly revised version was published in England in book form in April 1891, but the novel was reviewed in Britain after its appearance in Lippincott's. The addition of a preface, actually a lazy list of epigrams on the nature of art, artists and their creations, further alienated many readers and critics in an age when the moral message of any work of literature was of paramount importance. The reviews were damning – the book was denounced as immoral and their subtext was that perhaps Oscar was immoral too. W. H. Smith refused to stock the novel, on the grounds that it was 'filthy'. The *Daily Chronicle* wondered why Oscar had gone 'grubbing in muckheaps' and *Punch* used more elevated language to make the same point: 'A truer art would have avoided the … unsavoury suggestiveness which lurks in its spirit.'

Sin is a thing that writes itself across a man's face. It cannot be concealed.

The plot of the novel has often been described as Faustian, although there are no actual encounters with the devil. A portraitist, Basil Hallward, discusses with his friend Lord Henry Wotton the subject of the portrait he is working on, a beautiful and innocent young man named Dorian Gray. His interest piqued, Lord Henry asks to meet the young man. Hallward, who is in love with Dorian, demurs, finding something untoward in his friend's interest, but Lord Henry is at Hallward's house that afternoon when Dorian comes for his sitting, and he begins the process of subverting the young man's innocence and goodness. Oscar's ideas on beauty and art, particularly that they have no moral dimension, are voiced by Lord Henry in his reaction to Dorian's appearance:

> You have a wonderfully beautiful face, Mr Gray … And Beauty is a form of Genius – is higher, indeed, than Genius, as it needs no explanation. It is of the great facts of the world, like sunlight, or spring-time, or the reflection in dark waters of that silver shell we call the moon. It cannot be questioned. It has its divine right of sovereignty.

Lord Henry knows, through his philanthropic Aunt Agatha, that Dorian is a kind and charitable soul, but in the course of just a few hours, he skews the young man's perspective on the world and persuades him that the personal quest for pleasure should not be hampered by mere questions of good and evil.

Soon afterwards, Hallward finishes the portrait and delivers it to Dorian. Lord Henry continues to influence the young man and Dorian grows distant from Hallward, at one time his best friend.

Dorian falls in love with a beautiful and talented actress, Sybil Vane. When her involvement with Dorian prevents her concentrating on her acting career, he ends their relationship. When he next looks at his portrait it seems different – the change is subtle, but Dorian's angelic innocence has been replaced with an expression that is close to cruelty. He decides to take Sybil back but discovers that she has killed herself.

> Morality is simply the attitude we adopt towards people whom we personally dislike.

Moderation is a fatal thing. Enough is as bad as a meal. More than enough is as good as a feast.

In his distress, Dorian calls on Lord Henry, who lends him a decadent French novel, *The Yellow Book*, which is nothing less than a guide to the pursuit of sensual pleasure. Dorian begins to live life for himself, with no kindness or consideration towards others. Each time he behaves badly his portrait changes, becoming increasingly flawed. Dorian himself remains unchanged, and when he meets Hallward some years later at the age of 38, his youthful beauty has been unassailed by time. He invites Hallward to his home and shows him his ever-changing portrait, which by now is hidden in the attic. Hallward is horrified when he sees the extent to which the portrait has been corrupted by its subject's actions and he begs Dorian to repent while there is still time. Dorian pulls out a knife and stabs him to death, and arranges for the secret disposal of the corpse. He later has a chance encounter with Sybil's brother James, who is bent on revenge for his sister's suicide, and Dorian engineers his death too. Back in the attic, the portrait grows uglier and uglier.

Dorian, confronted with his portrait on a daily basis, makes an attempt to reform and resists the temptation to corrupt a young woman. On his return home he gazes on his ageless beauty in the mirror and smashes the glass. He visits the attic to see if his attempt at virtue has improved his portrait, but it looks even worse than before. Frustrated, he picks up the knife he had used to murder Hallward and slashes the portrait to ribbons. The servants hear a loud crash from the attic and, when they investigate, find an ugly, debauched-looking corpse on the floor, a knife protruding from its chest. The portrait of their master is on the wall, as serenely beautiful as the day it was painted. Closer inspection reveals the corpse to be that of their master.

On the face of it, the story does have a moral. The narcissistic youth who sells his soul for eternal youth receives his punishment in the end. But what shocked the public was the account of the corruption of innocence, and the strong homoerotic narrative underlying the plot. Hallward loves

Dorian and Lord Henry desires him. Although there are female characters (Lord Henry's wife, Sybil Vane), they are shadowy and inconsequential, at best two-dimensional. Oscar concentrated on developing his three male protagonists. He said that each of them represented a facet of his persona: 'Basil Hallward is what I think I am: Lord Henry what the world thinks me: Dorian is what I would like to be in other ages, perhaps.' Hallward was the creative artist, Wotton the witty conversationalist and Dorian the golden youth that Oscar might have wished to be.

When the reviewers savaged the novel some friends dropped Oscar and Constance, causing Constance to say, regretfully, 'Since Oscar wrote Dorian Gray, no one will speak to us.' However, most stood by them, believing that Dorian was the best thing Oscar had ever written. Lady Wilde, true to form, was in raptures: 'It is the most wonderful piece of writing in all the fiction of the day.' Oscar, who still enjoyed spending time in undergraduate circles at Oxford, had soon attracted quite a following of admiring young men. While writing the book he had started an affair with a 24-year-old poet, John Gray, and had named his main character after him, but now he became distracted by the adulation of his fans. In June, while at home in Tite Street, he was introduced by a friend to a Magdalen student who claimed to have read the novel 'fourteen times running' (he had actually read it a mere nine times). It was the first meeting between Oscar and Lord Alfred Douglas, youngest son of the Marquess of Queensberry. It was a case of life imitating art. Just as Basil Hallward had been smitten by Dorian Gray, so Oscar was instantly dazzled by the young man's angelic blond beauty.

Oscar worked hard to vindicate the underlying premise of Dorian. In July and September 1891 his essay 'The Critic as Artist' was published in the *Nineteenth Century*. In a discussion that turns the conventional notion of criticism on its head, Oscar states that a response informed by

Any preoccupation with ideas of what is right or wrong in conduct shows an arrested intellectual development.

When we are happy we are always good but when we are good we are not always happy.

societal norms of morality interferes with the proper aesthetic response to a work of art or literature. 'Aesthetics are higher than ethics. They belong to a more spiritual sphere.'

In February 1891 a second essay, 'The Soul of Man Under Socialism' was published in the *Fortnightly Review*. This was Oscar's take on the doctrine of socialism that was a hot topic of conversation in some intellectual circles, thanks to men of letters such as George Bernard Shaw and the members of the Fabian Society, which had been founded in 1884 to promote democratic socialism through societal reform. Oscar's view was anarchic and looked forward to the abolition not only of government, but also of marriage and family life, property ownership and, in an ideal world, jealousy. He justified the necessity of sin as 'an essential element of

Caricature of Oscar
with his work by
Aubrey Beardsley

progress'. 'Is this dangerous? Yes; it is dangerous – all ideas, as I told you, are so.'

Oscar's flirtation with the novel was over. With hardly any narrative prose and few descriptive passages, *Dorian Gray* is almost all dialogue – sparkling, witty dialogue – and begged to be staged. Perhaps it made Oscar realise that dramatic writing was more his genre. 'I can't describe action,' he wrote to a friend. 'My people sit in chairs and chatter.' His chattering people would soon set him on the road to lasting fame.

CHAPTER 10

The Playwright

NAZIMOVA
in Oscar Wilde's
"Salome"

I love acting.
It is so much
more real
than life.

Direction By CHARLES BRYANT
Sets and costumes by NATACHA RAMBOVA
Photographed By CHARLES VAN ENGER
Scenario By PETER M. WINTERS

Oscar, an assiduous theatre-goer and an enthusiastic if unsuccessful playwright, returned to writing for the stage. *The Duchess of Padua* had been a flop, but in 1889 a New York producer decided that it could be staged, with a few amendments and change of title. *Guido Ferranti* opened on Broadway in January 1891. It received fairly neutral reviews and ran for three weeks.

Back in London, Oscar hoped that the actor-manager George Alexander would stage the play there under its original title. Instead, Alexander asked Oscar to write a new play, and put up a £50 advance. Oscar began to formulate the idea for a social comedy called *A Good Woman*. Once he had established a plot the writing came easily to him. He boasted that he could write a play of that nature in one week and he rented a house in the Lake District so that he could concentrate on the work. It took him several weeks more than the single one he had predicted, but he had finished the play by October. He sent it to Alexander who pronounced it 'simply wonderful' and offered a fee of £1,000 for it. It was a lot of money, and Oscar was always cash strapped, but for once he showed some financial shrewdness. He wrote to Alexander, 'I have so much confidence in your judgement, that … I will take a percentage.' It was a calculated risk, but it paid off, and he ultimately received far more than £1,000 once the play went into production. He signed a contract with Alexander and then, suffering from nervous exhaustion, went to Paris for two months.

While there, he started writing a very different kind of play, on a subject that had fascinated him for quite some time – the biblical princess who had asked for the head of John the Baptist on a platter. Coincidentally, his Parisian friend, the poet Mallarmé, was also researching her and the two men had many conversations on the subject. The anti-heroine of *Salomé* is sensuous, enthralling and unscrupulous,

The play was a great success but the audience was a disaster.

> One should believe evil of everyone, until, of course, people are found out to be good. But that requires a great deal of investigation nowadays.

and Oscar had Sarah Bernhardt in mind for the title role. He had not quite finished the play when he returned to London for Christmas and went to the south coast for a few days to complete it before attending rehearsals in the New Year for *A Good Woman*, now retitled *Lady Windermere's Fan: A Play About a Good Woman*.

The plot of *Lady Windermere's Fan* revolves around family secrets and a confusion of identity, a theme to which Oscar would return. Lady Windermere suspects her husband is having an affair with an older woman, Mrs Erlynne. When confronted, Lord Windermere denies her accusation, but then invites the woman to his wife's birthday celebration. Lady Windermere, believing her suspicions to have been confirmed, takes a lover and leaves her husband, but Mrs Erlynne tries to persuade her to return to him. The denouement reveals Lord Windermere's 'lover' to be his wife's mother, who had abandoned her daughter 20 years earlier.

The play opened in St James's Theatre on 20 February 1892, to an audience packed with Oscar's friends and admirers, many of them sporting dyed green carnation buttonholes, at Oscar's request. The play was greeted enthusiastically and when called on stage after the performance the author told the delighted audience:

ST. JAMES'S THEATRE,
Sole Lessee and Manager - - Mr. GEORGE ALEXANDER.
Every Evening at 9 o'clock punctually,
A New and Original Play, in Four Acts, by OSCAR WILDE, entitled

Lady Windermere's Fan

Lord Windermere	Mr. GEORGE ALEXANDER
Lord Darlington	Mr. NUTCOMBE GOULD
Lord Augustus Lorton	Mr. H. H. VINCENT
Mr. Charles Dumby	Mr. A. VANE TEMPEST
Mr. Cecil Graham	Mr. BEN WEBSTER
Mr. Hopper	Mr. ALFRED HOLLES
Parker	Mr. V. SANSBURY
Lady Windermere	Miss WINIFRED EMERY
The Duchess of Berwick	Miss FANNY COLEMAN
Lady Plimdale	Miss GRANVILLE
Mrs. Cowper-Cowper	Miss A. DE WINTON
Lady Jedburgh	Miss B. PAGE
Lady Agatha Carlisle	Miss LAURA GRAVES
Lady Strutfield	Miss M. GIRDLESTONE
Rosalie	Miss W. DOLAN
Mrs. Erlynne	Miss MARION TERRY

ACTS I & IV.	Morning-Room at Lord Windermere's, Carlton House Terrace	(H. P. Hall)
ACT II.	Drawing-Room at Lord Windermere's	(Walter Hann)
ACT III.	Lord Darlington's Rooms	(W. Harford)

The Incidental Music by WALTER SLAUGHTER. The Furniture and Draperies by Messrs. FRANK GILES & Co., Kensington. The Dresses, &c., by Mesdames SAVAGE and PURDUE and Madame YORKE. The Wigs by Mr. C. H. FOX. The Etchings and Engravings in the corridors and vestibule kindly lent by Mr. I. P. MENDOZA, King Street, St. James's.

The actors have given us a charming rendering of a delightful play, and your appreciation has been most intelligent. I congratulate you on the great success of your performance, which persuades me to believe that you think almost as highly of the play as I do.

The play is light on plot, something that was picked up on in some reviews, but the general consensus was expressed by one critic, A. P. Walkley, who wrote that 'when a dramatist gives me such a perpetual flow of brilliant talk as Mr Wilde gives, I am willing to forgive him all the sins in the dramatic Decalogue, and the rest.'

Buoyed up by his success Oscar set about having *Salomé* staged. Sarah Bernhardt, looking to revive her slightly flagging career, agreed to play the title role. Oscar became involved in all the many details of stage and costume design. However, rehearsals of the play had been under way for a fortnight when Oscar became aware that the licensor of plays was considering banning it under the provisions of ancient legislation that prohibited the theatrical depiction of characters from the Bible. Oscar provoked much hilarity when he declared his intention to become a French citizen and have the play, which he had written in French rather than English, staged in Paris – male French citizens, even new ones, were required to report for military service; the cartoonists, predictably, had a field day. The play was banned in Britain – Shaw was one of its only supporters – and Oscar railed against a system of censorship that would ban a play but permit the exhibition of those same biblical characters in stone and on canvas. He had it published in a beautiful edition, but gave up on the prospect of a theatrical outing for it.

That summer, Oscar started work on a second comedy, renting a house in Norfolk as a workplace. He finished *A Woman of No Importance* in October. He had, somewhat reluctantly, promised the play to his old friend Herbert Beerbohm Tree, actor-

It is not good for one's morals to see bad acting.

The truth is rarely pure and never simple. Modern life would be very tedious if it were either, and modern literature a complete impossibility.

manager of the Haymarket Theatre. Even as he delivered it to Tree, Oscar expressed his reservations as to whether he was the right actor for the character of Lord Illingworth. Notwithstanding his concerns, the play went into rehearsal at the end of March 1893 and opened on 19 April.

Considered the weakest of Oscar's social comedies, *A Woman of No Importance* is a good example of a play where the 'people sit around chatting to each other', at least in the first act. The plot, again, revolves around an old secret that comes home to roost. Gerald Arbuthnot has his sights set on an American heiress, Hester, and has been offered the post of secretary to Lord Illingworth. However, it is soon revealed that Lord Illingworth is Gerald's father. He had refused to marry Gerald's mother, the unimportant woman of the title, when she became pregnant. Mrs Arbuthnot is horrified when she realises that her son's employer is her seducer. She refuses to allow Gerald to go on working for Lord Illingworth and Gerald is placed in the invidious position of choosing between his mother and his career. He tries to persuade Lord Illingworth to marry his mother, but when Mrs Arbuthnot learns of this she refuses to entertain the idea, and even refuses Lord Illingworth's offer to make a financial settlement in Gerald's favour. As the play draws to a close Gerald is about to become engaged to Hester and Lord Illingworth has no role to play in his life.

The play was a hit with audiences and most critics. *The Times* reported that it was 'fresh in ideas and execution and is written moreover with a literary polish too rare on the English stage.' The Prince of Wales urged Oscar not to 'alter a single line'. Oscar was delighted with his latest play's reception. When he encountered Arthur Conan Doyle one day he urged him to attend a performance with an encouragement that was pure Oscar: 'Ah, you must go. It is wonderful. It is genius.'

In late spring 1893 Oscar rented a large house in Goring-on-Thames, a place where he could entertain family and friends and write his next play, *An Ideal Husband*. The theme of this witty comedy, an examination of the consequences of political treachery, was very different from that of his previous two plays.

Sir Robert Chiltern, a cabinet minister, sold a state secret in his youth and his past catches up with him when he is blackmailed into supporting a fraudulent Argentine construction scheme. His blackmailer, Mrs Cheveley, has in her possession a letter that is proof of his crime. Chiltern's wife, who has no knowledge of her husband's youthful crime, applies impossibly high standards to him – she expects him to be morally upright, an ideal husband in every way – and she insists that he retract his support for the Argentine scheme. Chiltern's friend, Lord Goring, urges Robert to confess to his wife, and asks Lady Chiltern to be a little less rigid. Mrs Cheveley has been in love with Lord Goring for years and offers to exchange the letter that incriminates his friend for his promise to marry her. Lord Goring has other ideas, but it takes a series of misunderstandings, revelations and some sleight of hand to arrive at a happy ending for all.

'You brute! You coward!' from an anonymous artist's illustrations to Oscar Wilde's *An Ideal Husband,* 1907.

Geniuses are always talking about themselves when I want them to be thinking about me.

The move away from single mothers into the realm of blackmail is interesting. At this time Oscar was concerned that his homosexual activities, still secret, made him vulnerable to blackmail attempts.

The play, which had not been commissioned, was finished in early 1894. It was rejected by the Garrick Theatre, but was snapped up at the Haymarket by the actor-manager Lewis Waller, who took the title role for himself. The play opened on 3 January 1895 and was a hit with public and critics alike. George Bernard Shaw, one of Oscar's greatest admirers, wrote that 'Mr Wilde is to me our only thorough Playwright. He plays with everything: with wit, with philosophy, with drama, with actors and audience, with the whole theatre.'

Meanwhile, Oscar had been working hard. Perpetually short of money, despite the success of his plays, he needed to keep earning. He finished his long poem 'The Sphinx', begun so many years earlier on his trip to Paris with his mother, and had it published in a limited edition. He quipped that he had thought of printing only three copies: 'one for myself, one for the British Museum and one for Heaven. I had some doubts about the British Museum.' In August 1894 he rented a small house in Worthing for a family holiday and as a place to start work on another script. *The Importance of Being Earnest* would be his most successful play. He went to London in September with an outline and received an advance from the Garrick Theatre. He finished writing in October and the play went into rehearsal in January 1895, just as *An Ideal Husband* opened. Oscar had never been busier.

The play has all the elements of farce – an autocratic aunt, a clergyman, two young men about town with two make-believe friends, a governess and two beautiful young women. Jack Worthing loves Gwendolen Fairfax, but her cousin and his friend Algernon Moncrieff won't give his permission for them to marry until Worthing tells him about Cecily, whose name is inscribed on Worthing's cigarette case.

A cynic is a man who knows the price of everything and the value of nothing.

Worthing reveals that his adoptive father appointed him guardian to his granddaughter Cecily, who knows him as Uncle Jack. When Jack goes to London he pretends to be his imaginary brother Ernest. Gwendolen, quite arbitrarily, cannot love any man who is not called Ernest. Algernon meets Cecily and falls in love with her – she too wants to marry someone called Ernest.

Algernon's aunt, Lady Bracknell, won't countenance Jack's engagement to her daughter because the infant Jack was found in a handbag at a railway station and his parentage is unknown. Meanwhile, Jack and Algernon are conniving with the local clergyman to be rebaptised 'Ernest'. Cecily's governess, Miss Prism, is revealed to have been nurse to a family who mislaid her infant charge when she absent-mindedly put him in a handbag and deposited it in the left luggage at Victoria Station. The baby's mother was Lady Bracknell's sister, Algernon's mother, so Jack and Algernon are brothers, and Jack's real name is Ernest. The four young people are united and happiness is within reach.

The Importance of Being Earnest: A Trivial Comedy for Serious People opened on the evening of Valentine's Day, a fitting day for a frothy romantic comedy. The audience loved it and the theatre resounded with their laughter. Of all Oscar's plays it fulfilled his own criterion of 'art for art's sake'. Oscar wrote to Robbie Ross that the basic point of the play was 'that we should treat all trivial things very seriously, and all the serious things of life with sincere and studied triviality'. There is no moral message, and that upset some of the critics. 'What can a poor critic

She has the remains of really remarkable ugliness.

Evelyn Millard and Irene Vanbrugh in the 1895 London premiere of *The Importance of Being Earnest*.

If you think of anything you kill it. Nothing survives being thought of.

do with a play which raises no principle, whether of art or morals, creates its own canons and conventions, and is nothing but an absolutely wilful expression of an irrepressible personality?' wrote William Archer. However, the *New York Times* was ungrudging in its praise: 'Oscar Wilde may be said to have at last, and by a single stroke, put his enemies under his feet.'

With two comedies playing to packed London theatres, Oscar's career was at its zenith, but in his personal life storm clouds were gathering ominously overhead.

CHAPTER 11

Lord Alfred Douglas

The very essence
of romance is
uncertainty.

Lord Alfred Douglas, youngest son of the Ninth Marquess of Queensberry and known to his intimates as Bosie, met Oscar for the first time at the writer's house in Tite Street, shortly after the publication of *The Picture of Dorian Gray*. He had been captivated by the novel and was impressed by but not attracted to its author, who by this time was overweight and ungraceful, with a mouth full of badly arranged teeth. Oscar, on the other hand, was smitten with the slim and beautiful young man, and he brought him upstairs to meet Constance.

Bosie was flattered when Oscar, several days after that first meeting, invited him to dine at his club. He gave him a copy of the deluxe edition of his novel, inscribed

Alfred Douglas from his friend who wrote this book.
Oscar, July 91

Bosie was 21, still up at Oxford, and he was already a

practising homosexual. He made it a
rule to sleep only with boys who were
younger than him – looks aside, Oscar,
at 36, would not normally have been on
his radar. According to him, he eventually
succumbed because Oscar had 'laid siege'
to him. Oscar maintained otherwise – he
was always attentive to new acquaintances
who interested him, and that attention may
have been construed by Bosie as part of a
wooing process.

Lady Windermere's Fan opened in
February 1892 and shortly afterwards,
while Oscar was basking in the glow
of success, Bosie sought his help with a
blackmailer. Bosie was careless about his
illegal sexual adventures – perhaps he felt
that his title placed him above the law
– and he had allowed an incriminating
letter to fall in to the wrong hands. Oscar

I can resist
everything
except
temptation.
If your sins
find you out,
why worry! It
is when they
find you in,
that trouble
begins.

solved the problem by putting the matter in the hands of his lawyer and providing £100 to pay off the blackmailer. Bosie was impressed and soon they were constantly in each other's company. At that time Oscar was still involved with John Gray, but he gradually began seeing less of him, finally dropping him altogether. The non-committal inscription in *Dorian Gray* was superseded by the more fulsome one in the copy of *Poems* given to Bosie in June 1992:

> *From Oscar*
> *To the Gilt-mailed*
> *Boy*
> *At Oxford*
> *In the heart*
> *Of June*
> *Oscar Wilde*

In October Oscar went to Bracknell with Bosie to visit his mother. Lady Queensberry was worried about her son's lack of application at Oxford, and about his spendthrift ways. She believed he was vain and spendthrift and was frittering his life away. Indeed, he was frittering Oscar's money away – Oscar, always generous to a fault and feckless with money, was an easy target for Bosie. Later, Bosie wrote to Robbie Ross that he remembered very well 'the sweetness of asking Oscar for money. It was a sweet humiliation and exquisite pleasure to both of us.' He enjoyed being kept (when his father threatened to cut off his allowance he didn't make any attempt to discourage him, knowing that he could rely on Oscar's generosity) and assumed that Oscar enjoyed doing the keeping. Although Bosie could be charming and amusing, as their relationship proceeded Oscar began to tire of his violent temper and reckless behaviour.

For more than a year, from November 1892 to December 1893, Oscar and Bosie were constantly in each other's company. Oscar was besotted and wrote to Robbie

> Young men want to be faithful and are not; old men want to be faithless and cannot.

Lord Alfred Douglas, photographed as a student at Oxford, 1891.

Nothing looks so like innocence as an indiscretion.

Ross that 'he is quite like a narcissus – so white and gold … he lies like a hyacinth on the sofa, and I worship him'. He encouraged Bosie in his efforts at poetry and in his editorship of the Oxford magazine, *The Spirit Lamp*.

Despite their infatuation with each other, neither Oscar nor Bosie was exclusive. Oscar moved in the shady world of male brothels and rent boys in both London and Paris. He was popular because he treated the boys courteously, paid them well and even regaled them with amusing stories. He and Bosie would recount their sexual adventures to each other, swapping notes and, occasionally, boys. When they were together they flaunted their relationship, a dangerous thing to do given the criminality of their behaviour. Until now, Oscar had always managed to be discreet – he was

Lord Alfred Douglas, age 21, at Oxford

reasonably safe from prosecution as long as he kept a low profile. He often took rooms in hotels and he rented houses, ostensibly in order to work, but also so that he and Bosie (and other young men) could be together. Bosie was reckless, taking care never to use the side entrance of the hotels they stayed in, always hoping that his activities would come to the attention of his father, whom he loathed, because of his treatment of his mother, who had divorced him for adultery in 1887.

Queensberry was a difficult man with a temper as violent as his youngest son's. He was homophobic, anti-Christian and a bad poet. He constantly took his son to task for his failings, including his lack of academic progress at Oxford. In March 1893 Bosie began to take extra tutoring in an attempt to improve his performance but soon went off, tutor in tow, to stay with Oscar in a rented house at Babbacombe Cliff. He then went back to London with Oscar to stay at the Savoy, and in May Oscar came to Oxford on a long visit, reprising his own student days, and was in great demand as a dinner guest and raconteur. Bosie failed his final exams by failing to turn up for them. Magdalen College was not impressed and Bosie retorted

> Every impulse that we strive to strangle broods in the mind and poisons us … the only way to get rid of temptation is to yield to it.

that the disgrace was Magdalen's, not his. He then joined Oscar, who was writing *An Ideal Husband* in yet another rented house, this one at Goring-on-Thames. People dropped in and out all summer, including Oscar's eldest son, Cyril.

Oscar was dismayed by Bosie's failure to get his degree, aware of how it would affect his career prospects. The young lord said arrogantly that Shelley had managed without an Oxford degree and it was equally acceptable for him. In August, when Bosie flew into a rage, out of the blue, Oscar said, calmly, that it was time for them to end their relationship.

> We are spoiling each other's lives. You are absolutely ruining mine and evidently I am not making you really happy. An irrevocable parting, a complete separation is the one wise philosophic thing to do.

Bosie left after lunch the same day, but within three days was begging Oscar to allow him to return. Oscar was unable to resist his pleas.

Back in London in the autumn, Bosie was aimless – he couldn't go back to Oxford – so Oscar asked him to translate *Salomé* into English. He hadn't counted on Bosie's poor grasp of French and the translation was unacceptable. Bosie was furious to have his work criticised and Oscar again tried to seize the opportunity to end their relationship. Robbie Ross intervened on Bosie's behalf, at his request, and Oscar relented and took him back, yet again.

Meanwhile, Lord Queensberry was furious that Bosie had come down from Oxford without a degree and he blamed Oscar for his son's failure. He was in

Those who are faithful know only the trivial side of love; it is the faithless who know love's tragedies.

a temper anyway, as his eldest son, private secretary to the Foreign Minister, was rumoured to be having an affair with the minister, Rosebery. His middle son had married the daughter of a pious family, and his own second wife had sought an annulment soon after their marriage on grounds of impotence. He was looking for a scapegoat and Oscar fit the bill. He demanded that he stop seeing his youngest son. Meanwhile, Oscar was expressing some alarm at Bosie's mental state and was writing to Lady Queensberry in an attempt to find a solution.

Bosie seems to me to be in a very bad state of health. He is sleepless, nervous, and rather hysterical … His life seems to me aimless, unhappy and absurd.

He suggests that Bosie could be sent to stay with friends in Egypt, as a way of getting him away from London, where

… he will not come to any good, and may spoil his young life irretrievably, quite irretrievably.

I like to think myself his greatest friend so I write to you quite frankly to ask you to send him abroad to better surroundings. It would save him, I feel sure.

Oscar was at his most productive at this time, turning out four successful plays in as many years. With his capricious demands and angry outbursts, Bosie, no matter how amusing and affectionate he could be, was becoming a somewhat tiresome distraction. He had become embroiled in a scandalous liaison with a 16-year-old and both he and Oscar thought it best if he disappeared for a while. Lady Queensberry took Oscar's letter at face value and arranged for Bosie to stay in Egypt with her friends, the Cromers. Oscar was looking forward to a respite, then Bosie said he wouldn't go unless Oscar reconciled with him. Under pressure, Oscar agreed, and in the late summer of 1893 Bosie set off for Cairo.

With Bosie safely out of the way, Oscar could concentrate on his work and he finished writing *An Ideal Husband*. He

Caricature of Lord Queensberry.

Keep love in your heart. A life without it is like a sunless garden when the flowers are dead.

also finished two more plays, *A Florentine Tragedy*, which, like *The Duchess of Padua*, was written in blank verse, and *La Sainte Courtisane*. He sketched out the plot of *Lady Windermere's Fan* and sent it to a producer in August. Only then did he set to work on *The Importance of Being Earnest*.

Bosie, desperate for contact with Oscar, kept up a one-sided correspondence with him from his exile in Egypt, and it was only after he had begged Constance to intervene with her husband that Oscar condescended to send him a telegram:

Time heals every wound but for many months I will neither write to you nor see you.

Bosie went to Paris and sent Oscar a telegram saying that he would not be responsible for his actions if Oscar didn't meet him. Oscar knew that there had been suicides in Bosie's family (it is believed that Bosie may have been schizophrenic), so he relented and went to Paris where they were reconciled.

Back in London, Bosie and Oscar were spotted having lunch together by Lord Queensberry, who came over to their table and had an affable conversation with them. Later he wrote to Bosie telling him how unacceptable his fecklessness was and ordering his 'intimacy with this man Wilde' to stop, on pain of being cut off. His son, characteristically, flew into a rage and sent an intemperate reply. His father retaliated with a threat: 'If I catch you again with that man I will make a public scandal in a way you little dream of.' Oscar was concerned. Bosie thought it best to leave London and decided to go to Florence in April. Oscar joined him there, returning to London in June. Concerned about Queensberry's threat, he sought legal advice but took no action. Queensberry made an unannounced visit to Tite Street and Oscar later described the encounter in *De Profundis*.

In my library at Tite Street, waving his small hands in the air in epileptic fury, your father, with his bully, or his friend, between us, had stood uttering every foul word his foul mind could think of, and screaming the loathsome threats he afterwards with such cunning carried out.

Bosie's continued taunting of his father did nothing to defuse the situation, and Oscar's anxiety increased. Much later he told Bosie that 'the prospect of a battle in which you would be safe delighted you'. Oscar's lawyer, George Lewis, had been retained by Queensberry, so he was unable to advise him on how to proceed. Oscar engaged another lawyer, Travis Humphreys, who wrote to Queensberry and asked him to retract his libel. Queensberry refused, demanding that Oscar finish his association with Bosie. The situation calmed somewhat during the summer and Oscar was able to finish *The Importance of Being Earnest* in the small house in Worthing that he had rented. His entire family was there. Bosie visited and 'had great fun', although he was sensitive enough to realise that Constance wished him elsewhere.

In September 1894, *The Green Carnation*, a book by Robert Hitchens was published. It was a very obvious parody of Oscar and Bosie, and added fuel to Lord Queensberry's fire. Word went around that Oscar had written the book, an idea he refuted in a letter to the *Pall Mall Gazette*:

I invented that magnificent flower. But with the middle-class and mediocre book that usurps its strangely beautiful name I have ... nothing whatsoever to do. The flower is a work of art. The book is not.

Events began to gather their own momentum. During the summer some injudicious letters of Oscar's had fallen into Queensberry's hands. On 18 October 1894 Bosie's eldest brother died in circumstances that suggested suicide amid rumours of his involvement in a homosexual liaison with Lord Rosebery. Lord Queensberry, humiliated by the annulment on grounds of his impotence that had been granted his second wife on 20 October, began to plot his revenge on the homosexual seducer of his youngest son. He bought tickets for the opening night of *The Importance of Being Earnest* on 14 February 1895, with

It is only shallow people who require years to get rid of an emotion. A man who is master of himself can end a sorrow as easily as he can invent a pleasure.

True friends stab you in the front.

Lord Queensberry's infamous calling card.

One could never pay too high a price for any sensation.

the intention of denouncing Oscar publicly. Oscar told the theatre manager to return his money with a note that the play was sold out. However, his anxiety was increasing. On 18 February, Lord Queensberry left a card at Oscar's club. It read, 'To Oscar Wilde, posing Somdomite' [sic]. Oscar didn't receive it until his next visit to the club, 10 days later. Goaded beyond reason, Oscar wrote to Robbie Ross:

> Bosie's father has left a card at my club with hideous words on it. I don't see anything now but a criminal prosecution. My whole life seems ruined by this man.

He asked George Lewis what he should do, forgetting that he was acting for Queensberry. His advice would probably have been to tear up the card and forget about it. Ross gave the same advice, but Oscar had decided to make a legal response to the insult, setting the stage for the next devastating act of his life.

CHAPTER 12

Oscar's Trials

*With what a
crash this fell!*

THE WILDE v QUEENSBERRY CASE
AND HOW IT ENDED

Mr OSCAR WILDE
IN THE
WITNESS BOX

Mr CARSON QC CROSSEXAMINES
WILDE

PARKER
GIVING
EVIDENCE

ARREST OF WILDE AT THE CADOGAN HOTEL

TAYLOR JOINS WILDE
IN THE
DOCK

Sir EDWD CLARKE
DEFENDING
FOR THE
DEFENCE

LORD A DOUGLAS

AT THE OLD BAILEY

AT BOW STREET

IN THE POLICE CELL

On 1 March 1895 Oscar went to Great Marlborough Street police station with his solicitor, Travers Humphreys, and Bosie, and laid a charge of libel against Lord Queensberry. Queensberry was arrested the following day on the charge of 'contriving and maliciously intending to injure [Oscar Wilde] and to excite him to commit a breach of the peace and to bring him into public contempt scandal and disgrace'. *The Times* reported:

> At Marlborough Street on Saturday, the Marquess of Queensberry, aged 50, described as having no occupation and as residing in Carter's Hotel Dover St., was charged before Mr Newton on a warrant of defamatory libel concerning Mr Oscar Wilde on February 18th.

On 9 March Oscar arrived at the committal hearing in a carriage with a coachman and footman, accompanied by Bosie and Bosie's brother. He was met by crowds of people, all hoping for a place in the public gallery. Queensberry's lawyer said that he would be offering the defence of justification, implying that the alleged libel was true and that publishing it was in the public interest.

Oscar and Bosie decamped to Monte Carlo, returning on 25 March in time for the announcement of the trial date – 3 April. Queensberry had made use of the intervening weeks to gather evidence of Oscar's homosexual liaisons. Humphreys didn't delve very deeply into the protestations of innocence uttered by both Oscar and Bosie – otherwise he might, at that juncture, have brought pressure to bear on Oscar to drop the suit. On 30 March Queensberry's plea of justification was entered, and it included a list of 13 boys, 10 of whom were named, whom Oscar was accused of soliciting. It also relied on what it claimed was the inherent immorality of

It is perfectly monstrous the way people go about nowadays, saying things behind one's back that are absolutely and entirely true.

Lord Queensberry

Edward Carson,
Queensberry's
barrister.

The Picture of Dorian Gray. Oscar wanted the matter settled speedily and didn't ask for time in which to consider a defence to the justification. It was the first of many mistakes.

Oscar's friend and lawyer, George Lewis, had been retained by Queensberry, but his friendship with Oscar now prompted him to withdraw from the case. He was replaced by Edward Carson, an ambitious Irish barrister and an acquaintance of Oscar's from childhood and his days as an undergraduate at Trinity College. At 40, he was Oscar's exact contemporary, so when some of the first words of Oscar's testimony included the statement that he was two years younger, he knew that he was lying, and was able to challenge the reliability of his evidence.

Failing to realise that he was falling into a trap of his own making, Oscar treated the proceedings as if they were a theatrical performance, with him cast in the leading role. He couldn't resist the temptation to be witty, even when it began to backfire. Sir Edward Clarke, who had been retained as Oscar's barrister, saw no reason to believe that Oscar had lied about his innocence, and his examination of him was bland. Carson, however, having established that Oscar had lied about his age, asked him if he had ever kissed a particular young servant boy of Bosie's. Oscar's response played to the gallery: 'Oh no, never in my life. He was a particularly plain boy.' Carson picked away at him, asking him if he would refuse to kiss a boy merely because he was ugly. The direction the case was taking, coupled with the evidence of rent boys that had been gathered by Queensberry's private detective, persuaded Oscar to withdraw his prosecution, three days after the trial had begun. Despite this, the judge ruled that Queensberry had been justified in calling Oscar a sodomite. Oscar was left with a huge legal bill and a badly damaged reputation. There was also enough evidence to make the possibility of a criminal prosecution being brought against him highly likely. He wrote to the editor of the *Evening News*:

It would have been impossible for me to have proved my case without putting Lord Alfred Douglas in the witness-box against his father … Rather than put him in so painful a position I determined to retire from the case, and to bear on my own shoulders whatever ignominy and shame might result from my prosecuting Lord Queensberry.

That evening, Oscar was arrested and charged with indecency. He was remanded at Bow Street overnight. Robbie Ross went to the house at Tite Street and removed any incriminating documents; he then went to Bow Street but he wasn't allowed to see Oscar.

The scandal that had attached itself to him caused many of Oscar's friends to melt away. His name was removed from the playbills of the two plays that were running in London and audiences thinned out. He was pilloried in the press. Bosie had told Oscar that his legal bills for the libel suit would be covered by his mother and brother, but no money was forthcoming from either quarter. Queensberry forced the sale of the house at Tite Street in order to recoup his legal fees. Oscar was refused bail and was remanded at Holloway Prison until his trial. Bosie, avoiding prosecution because of his father's influence, visited him there. Oscar wrote to a friend:

> A slim thing, gold-haired like an angel, stands always at my side. His presence overshadows me. He moves in the gloom like a white flower.

Oscar's trial began on 26 April. It had been preceded by three hearings, on 6, 11 and 18 April. The evidence at the hearings was speculative, at best, a sordid litany of hotel maids, soiled hotel sheets and 'unnatural practices', provided by a succession of chambermaids and blackmailing rent boys. It transpired after the trial that many of the latter had been paid by Lord Queensberry to come forward. One of the witnesses was a young man who had blackmailed Oscar when, owing to Bosie's carelessness in leaving them in a coat

With regard to modern journalists, they always apologise to one in private for what they have written against one in public.

The public have an insatiable curiosity to know everything, except what is worth knowing.

pocket that he gave away, some of Oscar's letters to Bosie had fallen into his hands. The fact that Oscar had paid the blackmailer was adduced as evidence of his guilt.

Oscar was indicted on 25 counts of gross indecency and sodomy. Much to his disadvantage, Alfred Taylor, a known procurer of rent boys, was joined with him as co-defendant. In the early days of Oscar's relationship with Bosie, Taylor, a former pupil at Marlborough public school, had introduced Oscar to several young men. His connection with Oscar, though tenuous, was considered sufficient to have him added to the prosecution.

Oscar was defended by Sir Edward Clarke, who had waived his fee. The case was heard by Mr Justice Charles, known for his strong views on pederasty. When the trial opened Oscar looked thin and unwell and was wearing his hair much shorter than previously. The *New York Times* described him as 'careworn and anxious'. He admitted to knowing the witnesses, but said he had done nothing with them. When asked by prosecuting counsel to describe the 'Love that dare not speak its name', a phrase from one of Bosie's poems, he summoned all his eloquence for a soliloquy that caused the onlookers in the gallery to burst into spontaneous applause.

The 'Love that dare not speak its name' in this century is such a great affection of an elder for a younger man as there was between David and Jonathan, such as Plato made the very basis of his philosophy, and such as you find in the sonnets of Michelangelo and Shakespeare. It is that deep, spiritual affection that is as pure as it is perfect … It is beautiful, it is fine, it is the noblest form of affection. There is nothing unnatural about it. It is intellectual, and it repeatedly exists between an elder and a younger man, when the elder man has intellect, and the younger man has all the joy, hope and glamour of life before him. That it should be so the world does not understand. The world mocks at it and sometimes puts one in the pillory for it.

Oscar's barrister made a strong defence, maintaining that the evidence of blackmailers could not be relied on. If Oscar were guilty, he asked, why would he have drawn attention to himself by proceeding with his libel case against Lord Queensberry? However, in his summing up on 30 April the judge did not discount the testimony of the unreliable witnesses and listed four questions for the consideration of the jury, only two of which concerned Oscar. The jury was sent out and deliberated for just under four hours. When they came back they said they had been unable to reach a unanimous verdict. The judge ordered a new trial and refused to grant bail. Oscar's solicitor made a new bail application before a different judge and this time it was granted, set for £5,000, only half of which was allowed on Oscar's own recognisance. The remaining £2,500 had to be raised from friends and family. Most were unforthcoming, but Bosie's brother Percy and a philanthropic and non-judgemental clergyman provided the surety.

Oscar was released on bail on 7 May and had to find somewhere to stay. The hotel he booked into at St Pancras evicted him when the manager realised who he was. His brother

Willie reluctantly allowed him to stay at the house he shared with Lady Wilde, allocating him a camp bed in a corner. When some friends, the Leversons, became aware of Oscar's plight they offered him a place to stay, which he accepted gratefully, and he moved into their children's nursery on 18 May.

Robbie Ross, understanding better than Oscar the danger he was in, tried to persuade him to leave for France. Another friend even went to the lengths of chartering a yacht to take him away. But Lady Wilde and Bosie urged him to stay. Constance hoped to avoid further disgrace, but Speranza insisted that it was a matter of honour, and she was sure that her son would be vindicated. Bosie wrote to him from France:

I rely on you to misrepresent me.

Robbie Ross

> The evolution of man is slow. The injustice of man is great.

It seems too dreadful to be here without you, but I hope you will join me next week. Do keep up your spirits, my dearest darling.

The new trial, again with Alfred Taylor as co-defendant, began on 22 May. Clarke argued for, and won, a separate trial for Oscar. Taylor's trial was held first, and was despatched speedily with a guilty verdict on the same day. Then it was Oscar's turn. The same flimsy evidence was paraded before the jury. His counsel argued that as Oscar had been so little blackmailed by the long line of blackmailers giving evidence, it was plain that there was no real evidence against him. Anything that had

Taylor and Wilde in the dock together at Bow Street.

Mr Justice Wills

been presented in evidence was unsubstantiated. He summed up with a passionate defence of Oscar and his value to society:

> If you feel it your duty to say that the charges … have not been proved, then I am sure you will be glad that the brilliant promise which has been clouded by these accusations, and the bright reputation which was so nearly quenched in the torrent of prejudice … have been saved from your verdict from absolute ruin; and that it leaves him, a distinguished man of letters and a brilliant Irishman, to live among us a life of honour and repute, and to give in the maturity of his genius gifts to our literature of which he has given only the promise of his early youth.

On 25 May the judge, Mr Justice Wills, delivered his summing up, heavily weighted against Oscar, to the jury. After just over two hours, they returned to the court with a guilty verdict. Declaring that it was the worst case he had ever tried, Mr Justice Wills passed a sentence of two years' imprisonment with hard labour on both defendants. The whole proceedings had been a triumph of narrow Victorian morality over evidence.

When the sentence was passed somebody called out 'Shame!' Oscar turned pale and looked as if he might collapse. 'My God, my God!' he said. The judge gestured to the warders to take him down.

During his first trial, Oscar had written to Bosie:

My dearest boy,

This is to assure you of my immortal, my eternal love for you. Tomorrow all will be over. If prison and dishonour be my destiny, think that my love for you and this idea, this still more divine belief that you love me in return will sustain me in my unhappiness and make me capable, I hope, of bearing my grief most patiently.

The next two years of Oscar's life would be filled with grief and hardship.

We are each our own devil, and we make this world our hell.

Notice of the sale of Oscar Wilde's effects.

Suffering is one very long moment.

After Oscar's sentence had been handed down, the members of the press gallery left to file their accounts of the verdict and the Marquess of Queensberry hosted a celebratory dinner for his friends. Oscar was taken from the Old Bailey cells and brought to Holloway prison in a prison van, where, as a convicted prisoner who was not allowed to wear his own clothes, he was given a suit of prison clothing and a bonnet, all made of coarse cloth and patterned with arrows. A warder wrote down a detailed description of him, including any birthmarks and distinguishing features, then he had to take a bath (probably for delousing purposes) and submit to having his hair cut – his head was not quite shaved, but his hair was cut as close to the scalp as possible. He was assigned a number, which was how he was identified for the duration of his sentence. Holloway was a prison reserved for remand prisoners, so on 9 June Oscar was transferred to Pentonville. Having received a sentence of hard labour, he had to undergo a stringent medical examination to ensure that he was fit enough to carry it out. The prison rules were read out to him – this took an entire hour.

For the first month of his imprisonment Oscar had to spend six hours every day on a treadmill, with five minutes' rest every 20 minutes. His bed was a bare board – he would have to earn the right to a thin mattress. After the first four weeks his days on the treadmill were over and he was assigned another prison job – picking oakum. This was done by pulling old rope to bits – the shreds were then used as a

The two great turning points of my life were when my father sent me to Oxford and when society sent me to prison.

Prisoners on a treadmill.

213

All authority is quite degrading. It degrades those who exercise it, and it degrades those over whom it is exercised.

strengthener for caulk. It was mindless work and ripped the workers' hands to shreds. Oscar was allowed one hour's exercise every day, which was spent walking in the prison yard in single file with other prisoners. No prisoner was allowed to speak to another. Daily attendance at chapel, twice on Sundays, was mandatory.

For the first three months Oscar was not allowed to have any contact with the outside world. He had no writing materials and the only books allowed were a bible and a copy of *The Pilgrim's Progress*. The food was dreadful – gruel, bread, potatoes and inferior meat – and most of the prisoners had diarrhoea. The authorities, concerned that plumbing pipes would provide a means of communication between prisoners, had had all the toilets disconnected, and the prisoners had to spend the night in their cells with a tin can containing their own waste. Contemporary accounts provide graphic details of the horrendous stench of the overflowing containers. Many of the guards vomited when they opened the cell doors in the morning.

The punishing regime and dreadful food meant that Oscar quickly lost a substantial amount of weight. For a gregarious, talkative man who loved to read and write down his thoughts, the deprivation of human company, books and pen and paper must have been incalculably awful. One day, a prisoner who could speak without moving his lips said to him in the exercise yard, 'I am sorry for you: it is harder for the likes of you than it is for the likes of us.' In *The Ballad of Reading Gaol* Oscar remembered the dreadful nature of prison life:

HM Prison Reading, England, opened to the public in 2016 – exterior of preserved door to Oscar Wilde's cell.

It is not the prisoners who need reformation, it is the prisons.

We tore the tarry rope to shreds
With blunt and bleeding nails;
We rubbed the doors, and scrubbed the
*   floors,*
And cleaned the shining rails:
And, rank by rank, we soaped the plank,
And clattered with the pails.
We sewed the sacks, we broke the stones,
We turned the dusty drill:
We banged the tins, and bawled the hymns,
And sweated on the mill.

After three months Oscar was allowed to write and receive one letter, and have three 20-minute visits in the presence of a warder, separated from his visitors by a wire mesh. This could be repeated every three months. From the beginning, he was allowed a visit from a chaplain as often as he requested, and a daily visit from the prison governor. A Home Office visitor would see him once a month and, indeed, his first outside visitor

Sir Richard Haldane

was a member of a Home Office committee for the investigation of prisons, Sir Richard Haldane. After submitting Oscar to a moralising lecture Haldane urged him to use his experience in his writing. He also promised him that he would try to have some books sent to him. The governor objected but the Secretary of State had given his permission and the books duly arrived.

In July Oscar was transferred to Wandsworth Prison, a place known for its harsh regime and the brutality of its warders. He was visited there by Constance's brother, Otho Lloyd Holland, who told Oscar that his sister wanted a divorce. Oscar was distraught and he asked his old friend Robert Sherard to write to Constance begging her to consider a reconciliation. Constance agreed, and wrote to the governor of Wandsworth asking if she could visit Oscar. She came to see him on 21 September and promised him that he could join her and their sons when he came out of prison. She decided, however, to change her surname to Holland, taking the name that had been assumed by her brother in an attempt to evade his creditors.

In the meantime Sherard had been to Wandsworth, where

he had found Oscar thin, depressed and tearful. He had a sparse beard and his fingers were torn and bleeding. Sherard had some bad news for Oscar – Bosie, enjoying life on Capri, was planning to publish some of Oscar's letters to him in the *Mercure de France*. Oscar had had time to reflect on the fact that it was Bosie's inflammatory behaviour towards his father that had sent his lover down the road to ruin and he begged Sherard to stop him. He knew that Constance, wavering in her demand for a divorce, would have no hesitation in proceeding if the letters were published. Sherard made representations to the publisher, who asked Bosie if he wanted to recall the letters from publication. Bosie's response was a testament to his narcissism:

> I am the nearest and dearest friend of Mr Oscar Wilde, and the injuries and insults and practical social ruin which I have endured entirely on account of my steadfast devotion to him are too well known to make it necessary to recall them.

On 24 September and 12 November Oscar was released from prison to attend bankruptcy proceedings instigated by Lord Queensberry. He passed the intervening weeks in the prison infirmary, suffering from dysentery and an ear infection that had resulted from a fall in the prison chapel when he had fainted. When Haldane next visited he was alarmed by Oscar's condition and arranged to have him transferred to Reading Gaol.

On 21 November, instead of travelling in a prison van, Oscar was transferred to Reading by train, which involved a change at Clapham Junction. Handcuffed and wearing his prison uniform he had to stand for half an hour on the platform of a busy commuter station. It was agonising for him. People recognised him and jeered, and one man spat in his face. Later Oscar wrote of the incident:

> From two o'clock till half past two on that day I had to stand on the centre platform at Clapham Junction in convict dress and handcuffed, for the world to look at … Of all possible objects I was

One of the many lessons that one learns in prison is that things are what they are and will be what they will be.

Oscar Wilde in convict garb.

Prison life makes one see people and things as they really are. That is why it turns one to stone.

the most grotesque. When people saw me they laughed. Each train as it came in swelled the audience. Nothing could exceed their amusement … For half an hour I stood there in the grey November rain surrounded by a jeering mob.

The governor at Reading, Henry Isaacson, was an enthusiastic apologist for the Prison Act of 1865, which advocated that the best treatment for prisoners was 'hard labour, hard board and hard fare.' He was a stickler for order and detail and privileges were revoked for even the smallest infractions of the absurd prison rules. However, as Oscar was clearly unfit for any more hard labour, he was given work in the prison garden and library and he was even allowed to spend time reading, although writing was restricted to just a few letters a month. The prison library had a copy of an Italian primer,

Oscar Wilde's cell in HMS Prison Reading as it is today.

and he decided to teach himself Italian, realising that a future in Britain after his release was out of the question, given his notoriety.

On 19 February 1896 Constance visited Oscar again to tell him that his mother had died two weeks earlier. Lady Wilde had asked if Oscar could visit her before she died, but her request was refused. Oscar was devastated but not surprised, having had, he said, a visit from the banshee. Afterwards Constance wrote to Otho that Oscar looked 'a complete wreck'.

Oscar may have been out of the public eye, but he hadn't been forgotten. There were several petitions for his early release, although they fell on deaf ears. And there was also some encouraging news. Although the two plays running in London at the time of his trials had been taken off, in May 1895 'The Soul of Man Under Socialism' was reissued by Hatchards as 'The Soul of Man', and a new edition of *The Picture of Dorian Gray* was published that October. In February 1896 *Salomé* opened in Paris, and the 'triumphant performance' was enthusiastically received.

In July, there was a change for the better in Oscar's prison life. Isaacson was replaced as prison governor by James Nelson, who was influenced by the movement for prison reform that began in the 1890s. He took a more modern and humane approach to the prisoners in his charge. Oscar would later refer to him as 'a Christ-like man'. Nelson, understanding that writing was a form of therapy for Oscar, extended his letter-writing privileges so that he was able to write a long memoir (50,000 words) in the form of a letter to Bosie. He worked on this between January and March 1897. He was not allowed to keep the work in progress in his cell and he was not allowed to send it to anyone, although the governor gave it to him when he was released. As a letter it had no title, but Robbie Ross later suggested *De Profundis*. It was a form of confession in which he took responsibility for the extravagant and careless lifestyle that had led to his incarceration.

I must say to myself that I ruined myself, and that nobody great or small can be ruined except by his own hand. I am quite ready to say so. I am trying to say so, though they may not think it at the present moment. This pitiless indictment I bring without pity against myself. Terrible as was what the world did to me, what I did to myself was far more terrible still.

The gods had given me almost everything. But I let myself be lured into long spells of senseless and sensual ease. I amused myself with being a flâneur, a dandy, a man of fashion. I surrounded myself with the smaller natures and the meaner minds. I became the spendthrift of my own genius, and to waste an eternal youth gave me a curious joy. Tired of being on the heights, I deliberately went to the depths in the search for new sensation … I grew careless of the lives of others. I took pleasure where it pleased me, and passed on. I forgot that every little action of the common day makes or unmakes character, and that therefore what one has done in the secret chamber

Society often forgives the criminal; it never forgives the dreamer.

> As one reads history, one is absolutely sickened, not by the crimes that the wicked have committed, but by the punishments that the good have inflicted.

one has some day to cry aloud on the housetop. I ceased to be lord over myself. I was no longer the captain of my soul, and did not know it. I allowed pleasure to dominate me. I ended in horrible disgrace. There is only one thing for me now, absolute humility.

While he was writing, Oscar's awareness of the extent of Bosie's selfishness and careless self-interest crystallised. During and after Oscar's bankruptcy hearings Bosie had come to realise, through friends, that Oscar no longer cared for him as he once had. In May 1896 he had asked for Oscar's permission to dedicate a volume of poems to him. He was refused. It was the ultimate rejection. Oscar asked Robbie Ross to retrieve from Bosie everything that he had ever given him. Without a thought for Oscar's sufferings in prison Bosie wrote to a mutual friend from his comfortable lodgings in Capri:

I am not in prison but I think I suffer as much as Oscar and in fact more ... Doesn't he think that my life is just as much ruined as his and so much sooner?

In July 1896 there was an incident at the prison that formed the basis of Wilde's most famous poem. A 30-year-old man, Charles Thomas Wooldridge, was hanged for the murder of his wife. In *The Ballad of Reading Gaol* Oscar described the effect of the execution on the prison population:

There is no chapel on the day
On which they hang a man:
The Chaplain's heart is far too sick,
Or his face is far too wan,
Or there is that written in his eyes
Which none should look upon.
So they kept us close till nigh on noon,
And then they rang the bell,
And the Warders with their jingling keys
Opened each listening cell,
And down the iron stair we tramped,
Each from his separate Hell.
Out into God's sweet air we went,

To become a spectator of one's life is to escape the suffering of life.

Letter requesting Oscar's release.

226

But not in wonted way,
For this man's face was white with fear,
And that man's face was grey,
And I never saw sad men who looked
So wistfully at the day.

The final months of Oscar's incarceration passed slowly and drearily. He had made a friend of one of the warders and the other prisoners treated him as something of a celebrity, but liberation was the thing he desired most. His release date was 19 May. His request to bring the date forward by a few days so that he might avoid the attentions of the press was refused. He had been allowed to grow his hair for five months and he was given his own clothes for the journey from Reading to Pentonville – the rules dictated that he be released from the prison in which he was first incarcerated. On 18 May the governor gave him his manuscript of *De Profundis* and he left Reading Prison in a cab with two officers. This time, as he waited on the platform with his guards, he was not handcuffed. He spent the final night of his imprisonment at Pentonville, from where he emerged at 6.15 the following morning, a free man.

Oscar's release from prison.

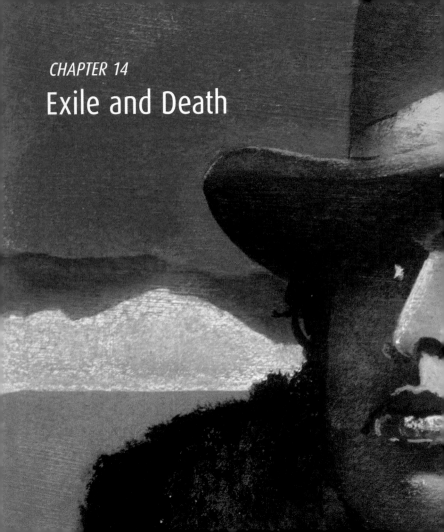

CHAPTER 14

Exile and Death

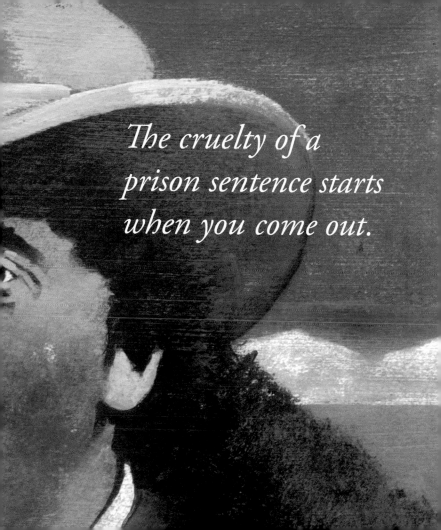

The cruelty of a prison sentence starts when you come out.

Oscar was met outside Pentonville by two of the friends who had stuck by him, More Adey and Stewart Headlam. They avoided the two members of the press who had turned up and went to Headlam's house, where they were joined by the Leversons. Oscar was relaxed and talkative and he looked better than he had during his trials.

One of the things that had troubled him during the last months of his imprisonment was the problem of where to stay. The house at Tite Street had been sold and no hotel would take him. That morning he sent a message to the Jesuits at Farm Street, proposing that he make a six-month retreat there. Unsurprisingly, they demurred. Oscar's back-up plan was to go to the Continent, so he took the afternoon train to Newhaven for the ferry to Dieppe. His old friends Reggie Turner and Robbie Ross met him in Dieppe the following morning. Oscar immediately entrusted his prison manuscript to Ross, asking him to keep the original and have two copies made, one to be sent to Bosie and one to himself.

Ross had raised £800 for Oscar to cover his expenses for the first period of his freedom. He checked into the Hotel Sandwich in Dieppe under the name Sebastian Melmoth, an alias he had agreed with Ross beforehand. He had told Bosie he didn't want to see him, but that he could write to him, and a letter arrived almost as soon as he had arrived at the hotel. Bosie had not yet read *De Profundis*, and although he knew that Oscar's feelings towards him had altered he was not aware of the extent to which they had changed. He presented himself as the most faithful of Oscar's friends, and accused Oscar of being ungrateful. Oscar still refused to see him, even though Bosie asked him to live with him for the rest of his life. Oscar continued to write to him, although he was still keeping him at arm's length.

There is only one thing in the world worse than being talked about, and that is not being talked about.

There is always something ridiculous about the emotions of people whom one has ceased to love.

Oscar was too recognisable to hide successfully behind an alias. He was snubbed on the streets and barred by the proprietors of the local eating establishments. After a week he decide to rent a house in a nearby village. He needed to get down to work – his profligate spending was a trait that remained and £800 wouldn't last long. His only other income was £200 per annum from Constance's marriage portion. His first mission was a series of letters to the press on the subject of prison reform. He thought he might write another play, and he was formulating a poem about his prison experiences. *The Ballad of Reading Gaol* is a long and harrowing reflection on daily prison life as well as events during his time in prison – an execution, a flogging, the weeping of imprisoned children. It is graphic, philosophical and spiritual. The first draft was completed in August.

I know not whether Laws be right,
Or whether Laws be wrong;
All that we know who lie in gaol
Is that the wall is strong;
And that each day is like a year,
A year whose days are long.
But this I know, that every Law
That men have made for Man,
Since first Man took his brother's life,
And the sad world began,
But straws the wheat and saves the chaff
With a most evil fan.
This too I know – and wise it were
If each could know the same –
That every prison that men build
Is built with bricks of shame,
And bound with bars lest Christ should see
How men their brothers maim.
With bars they blur the gracious moon,
And blind the goodly sun:
And they do well to hide their Hell,
For in it things are done
That Son of God nor son of Man
Ever should look upon!

Oscar now began to soften towards Bosie and agreed to meet him in Rouen for a reunion that was, inevitably, passionate. Until now Constance and Oscar had hoped to revive their family life, but the rekindling of his affair with Bosie dashed that aspiration. Oscar couldn't help himself. He wrote to Robbie Ross that a renewal of his relationship with Bosie was 'psychologically inevitable … I must love and be loved, whatever price I pay for it'. He left France and joined Bosie in Naples. In a rented villa he worked to finish his long poem and had it accepted for publication in London. Until he received any income from his writing, Oscar lived on his annual £200 from Constance, while Bosie had an allowance of over £1,000 from his mother. Both women threatened to stop the allowances if the affair continued and Lady Queensberry offered Oscar a lump sum of £200 if he promised to stop seeing her son. Bosie went to Rome in December, leaving Oscar in Naples, and they never lived together again. Oscar's reconciliation with Bosie, brief though it had been, had alienated Constance irrevocably. Oscar never again saw his sons, now renamed Holland.

Oscar having lunch with Bosie near Dieppe in 1898.

When I was young I thought that money was the most important thing in life; now that I am old I know it is.

In February 1898 Oscar moved to Paris to a hotel on the Left Bank. Although he was ostracised or ignored by many of his former friends and acquaintances, he had some friends in the city and he enjoyed Parisian café society. His funds were getting very low, but *The Ballad of Reading Gaol*, published anonymously on 9 February (it was attributed to 'C.3.3.', the number of his cell at Reading, although everyone knew the identity of the author; the seventh impression, printed in 1899, bore his own name), was selling well, so he had some income and, as a generous man himself in good times, he was happy to sponge off his friends. The poem was attracting a lot of reviews, most of them favourable, others non-committal at worst. It was published in France towards the end of 1898. Although Oscar was still working he no longer took

Snapshot of Oscar, probably taken by Bosie, spring 1900.

> I love scandals about other people, but scandals about myself don't interest me. They have not got the charm of novelty.

any joy in it. He edited the scripts of *An Ideal Husband* and *The Importance of Being Earnest*, a project that was long overdue, and had them published in book form.

Apart from his writing, Oscar's life in Paris was that of an indolent gentleman. He rose after noon, in the tradition of Lady Wilde, usually dined out, and consumed a lot of alcohol throughout the day. When he encountered old acquaintances he usually asked them for money. Any money he was given disappeared immediately – he had lived extravagantly all his life and was not inclined to change his ways to suit his much reduced circumstances. He embarked on a fond and uncomplicated relationship with a handsome young soldier, Maurice Gilbert, and he is known to have picked up rent boys on a regular basis.

In April 1898 Constance died in her adopted city of Genoa at the age of 40 after an operation on her spine, which had troubled her for years after a fall. Oscar was saddened but not grief-stricken. He regretted the fact that his chance of becoming reconciled with his family had died with her. His annual allowance was reduced to £150, enough to live on modestly, but at least it now had no conditions attached. He was not granted access to his sons.

In the spring of 1899 Oscar went to stay with a rich but parsimonious acquaintance in Switzerland, 'that dreadful place – so vulgar with its big ugly mountains', where he had the news that his brother Willie had died on 13 March. He was 46, and although they had been estranged for many years, his passing meant that Oscar was the sole survivor of the Merrion Square Wildes. He was not enjoying himself in Switzerland and he decided to go to Italy to boost his spirits. He visited Constance's grave in Genoa and in Rome he was blessed by Pope Leo XIII, afterwards claiming that the papal intervention had cured him of a skin rash. A number of his friends had converted to

> Catholicism is the only religion to die in.

Catholicism and he revived, briefly, his old flirtation with the Roman faith.

When he returned to Paris he found a cheap but convenient hotel whose proprietor indulged Oscar – he made no objection to his entertaining young men in his rooms and was not too unhappy when his bills weren't paid on time. He provided breakfast, lunch and a good supply of brandy. Oscar usually dined out, often alone. Although Bosie spent a lot of time in Paris he was not a part of Oscar's life there, although they saw each other occasionally. Lord Queensberry had died and Bosie was quickly going through his inheritance to fuel his gambling habit. Oscar, who had been so generous to him before his disgrace, asked him for some money, but Bosie refused on the selfish grounds that he needed it all for himself.

In 1900 Oscar's health began to deteriorate. He was growing very deaf and was plagued by skin rashes. He developed an abscess in the ear he had injured while in prison. It began to ooze a noxious discharge and in September he underwent an operation that was carried out in his hotel room. He never really recovered from the procedure. Robbie Ross came to stay with him during what Oscar was convinced was a fatal illness. He had good days and bad days, but he became gradually worse as October wore on. He was certain that he wouldn't live to see the dawn of the 20th century – by his reckoning that would be on 1 January 1901 – and had become morbidly fascinated by his impending demise. He asked Robbie Ross to make sure that *De Profundis* was published after his death. He was taking morphine and opium to cope with the pain and he drifted in and out of consciousness.

Towards the end he asked for a Catholic priest and was received into the church that had had such an attraction for him for so much of his life. He was so ill that he was unable to speak to the priest, and could only signal with his hand. In

Would you like to know the great drama of my life? It is that I have put my genius into my life – I have only put my talent into my works.

the afternoon of 30 November he died. The death certificate gave the cause of death as meningitis.

Bosie was notified by Robbie Ross and came to the requiem mass at St-Germain-des-Prés on 3 December. There were few other mourners – only four carriages followed the hearse – although many who were unable to be there had sent wreaths. Oscar was buried in Bagneux Cemetery. His simple headstone had a quotation from the Book of Job:

Oscar Wilde RIP

October 16th 1854 – November 30th 1900

Job xxix Verbis meis addere nihil audebant

Et super illos stillebat eloqiuem meum.*

*To my words they durst add nothing, and my speech dropped upon them.

In 1905 Robbie Ross arranged for the posthumous publication of *De Profundis*. Oscar's castigation of Bosie, for his greed, his egotism and his ingratitude, is powerful. It is hard to imagine that Bosie, who by then had married, fathered a child and renounced homosexuality, could have failed to be chastened by the angry prose of the letter, particularly Oscar's declaration that 'you were the absolute ruin of my art'.

Nine years after Oscar's death Ross had his remains moved to their final resting place, the Père Lachaise cemetery in Paris. When Ross died in 1918 his own ashes were placed in the tomb, at his request. An enduring monument to Oscar's life and work, Jacob Epstein's modernist *Winged Angel* was erected over the tomb. The inscription is from *The Ballad of Reading Gaol*:

The true artist is the man who believes absolutely in himself, because he is absolutely himself.

And alien tears will fill for him
Pity's long-broken urn,
For his mourners will be outcast men
And outcasts always mourn.

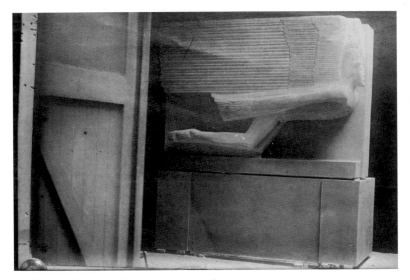

Jacob Epstein's memorial to Oscar, in its packing case.

The memorial *in situ*
in the Père Lachaise
cemetery in Paris.

CHAPTER 15
Oscar's Legacy

I shall never make a new friend in my life, though perhaps a few after I die.

During his lifetime Oscar was ridiculed and pilloried for his outrageous attitudes, his flamboyant dress sense, his belief that beauty trumped morality, and, ultimately, his refusal to deny or renounce the 'love that dare not speak its name'. However, his posthumous fame increased exponentially. Over a century after his death his witty aphorisms pepper people's conversations, his children's stories are still in publication, his four ostensibly light drawing-room comedies are staged regularly and he has been the subject of countless biographies and tributes. It is, however, in his polemical writing, notably 'The Soul of Man Under Socialism', that his soaring intellect and modern political outlook are apparent. With the exception of his long prison poem, *The Ballad of Reading Gaol*, much of his poetry seems overblown by today's standards and has not found a permanent place in hearts and minds in same the way as the verse of Wordsworth, Shelley and Keats.

248

Larger than life both physically and intellectually, a gregarious and brilliant conversationalist, Oscar was not given to hiding in the shadows and he never failed to impress his personality upon his contemporaries, for good or ill. His friend Charles Ricketts said of him that '[I]n intellect and humanity he is the largest type I have come across. Other greater men in my time were great in some one thing, not large in their very texture.' The novelist Henry James had a low opinion of him as a 'fatuous cad', but George Bernard Shaw, a great wit himself, said that Oscar would be his first choice 'for entertaining conversation by a first-class raconteur'. Oscar's prosecution for gross indecency and sodomy would probably not have proceeded had it not been for his iconoclastic propensities and his habit of not taking the authorities seriously. He was a proponent of

We can have in life but one great experience at best, and the secret of life is to reproduce that experience as often as possible.

249

the idea that people should be free to behave as they wished, and to express themselves in whatever manner they wished, as long as their actions were not harmful to others. It is not surprising that the strait-laced, law-loving Victorians regarded him as a corrupt and corrupting influence. Had he been a less prominent presence on the social stage he might never have ended up in court, defending what was, in those narrow times, the indefensible.

Whatever the reasons for Oscar's criminal conviction, ostensibly it was for the crime of homosexual activity, and he is considered to have suffered for his homosexuality rather than the perceived defects of his personality. As the second half of the 20th century progressed he became a gay icon, although he had never been a gay activist. In the United Kingdom male homosexual acts were partially decriminalised in 1967, and on 31 January 2017 Oscar was one of almost 50,000 gay men who received posthumous pardons under 'Turing's Law', so called after Alan Turing, pardoned in 2013 for his 1952 conviction for homosexual activity. Same-sex sexual activity was decriminalised in Ireland in 1993. This was the result of a campaign by Senator David Norris and the Campaign for

Homosexual Law Reform which led to a ruling in 1988 that Irish laws prohibiting male homosexual activities were in contravention of the European Convention on Human Rights.

From 5–17 October 2017, Oscar featured in Tate Britain's 'Queer British Art 1861–1967', an exhibition of art and artefacts spanning the era during which homosexuality was criminalised in Britain. A full-length portrait of a young and confident Oscar, painted in the early 1880s by Robert Goodloe Harper Pennington, was displayed beside Lord Queensberry's inflammatory calling card and the door to Oscar's cell, C. 3. 3, from the prison at Reading, a starkly graphic juxtaposition that illustrates the dreadful consequences of being a practising homosexual in Britain in less enlightened times.

One's past is what one is. It is the only way by which people should be judged.

Oscar Wilde, one of the greatest of men, clever, amusing, generous and kind, might, at the end of his life, seem to have failed, but his legacy says otherwise. Words were his currency and these have immortalised him. His personality shines through in everything he wrote and now, after more than a century, history remembers him kindly.

Personal experience is a most limited and vicious circle.

One can survive anything nowadays, except death, and live down anything except a good reputation.

Portrait of Oscar Wilde at the age of 27 by Robert Goodloe Harper Pennington.

Select Bibliography

Ellmann, Richard, *Oscar Wilde*, London: Hamish Hamilton 1987.

Fryer, Jonathan, *Wilde*, London: Thistle Publishing, 2013.

Holland, Merlin, & Harte-Davis, Rupert (eds.) *The Complete Letters of Oscar Wilde*, London: Fourth Estate, 2000.

Moyle, Franny, *Constance: The Tragic and Scandalous Life of Mrs Oscar Wilde*, London: John Murray Publishers (an Hachette UK Company), 2011.

The Collected Works of Oscar Wilde, Hertfordshire: Wordsworth Editions Limited, 1977.

Wright, Thomas, *Oscar's Books: A Journey around the Library of Oscar Wilde*, London: Chatto & Windus, 2008.

Oscar the Apostle, Puck's 'Wilde' dream for an Aesthetic future for America.

Picture credits

The publisher gratefully acknowledges the following image copyright holders. All images are copyright © individual rights holders unless stated otherwise. Every effort has been made to trace copyright holders, or copyright holders not mentioned here. If there have been any errors or omissions, the publisher would be happy to rectify this in any reprint.

p1   Sarony, Library of Congress
p2   Sarony, Library of Congress
p7   Shutterstock / Attila Jandi
p9   Wilde, William Royal College of Physicans Ireland
p11   National Gallery of Ireland
p13   Heritage Image / Alamy
p18   Teapot Press
p21   National Gallery of Ireland
p22   Shutterstock / Everett Historical
p25   Skärmavbild vilaer.se
p27   Teapot Press
p32   Shutterstock/ Matteo Provendola
p35   Magdalen College Founders Tower and Cloisters, Oxford
p39   William Wilde RCPI Heritage Centre
p40   Shutterstock / Everett Historical
p43   Sarony, Library of Congress
p45   Chronicle / Alamy
p47   Teapot Press
p52   Punch / University of Heidleberg
p56   Shutterstock / Everett Historical
p61   Sarony / Library of Congress
p66   Teapot Press
p71   Library of Congress
p72   Guion Bjorn Larsson / Timetable Images.com
p73   Classic Image / Alamy

p74   Sarony, Library of Congress
p75   Sarony, Library of Congress
p79   Sarony, Library of Congress
p79   Sarony, Library of Congress
p83   Sarony, Library of Congress
p91   Art Institute of Chicago
p93   Sarony, Library of Congress
p101 Wiki
p102 Wiki.es
p105 Rice University
p106 Sarony, Library of Congress
p110 Wikimedia
p113 Art Collection / Alamy
p117 Granger / Alamy
p123 Alamy
p124 Library of Congress
p128 Wiki / Brooklyn Museum Costume Collection at The Metropolitan Museum of Art
p131 Teapot Press / Wiki
p133 Wiki
p139 Teapot Press
p142 Teapot Press
p145 Teapot Press
p148 Wikimedia
p157 Wikimedia
p158 Library of Congress
p163 NY Library
p169 Complete Writings of Oscar Wilde
p173 Wikimedia
p175 Mary Evans

p175 National Portrait Gallery
p181 Alamy / Granger
p182 Teapot Press
p187 Wiki / Vanity Fair
p192 Wiki
p193 National Portrait Gallery
p194 Sarony, Library of Congress
p197 Teapot Press
p198 Teapot Press
p205 Wiki
p206 Bridgeman
p207 Teapot Press
p209 Wiki
p211 Shutterstock
p213 Wiki
p215 wyrdlight/Alamy
p216 Wikimedia
p217 Mary Evans
p220 Wiki
p225 Wiki
p226 Mary Evans
p227 Illustrated Police News
p228 Mary Evans
p234 Buruma
p236 National Portrait Gallery
p244 Bain / Library of Congress
p245 Shutterstock
p246 National Portrait Gallery
p252 Library of Congress
p253 William Andrews Clarke Memorial Library
p254 Library of Congress